THE ESSENTIAL HANDBOOK
FOR EMERGING WOMEN IN BUSINESS & LEADERSHIP

Compiled By
Shawette Mitchell

Propel: The Essential Handbook for Emerging Women in Business & Leadership

Copyright © 2019 by Sharvette Mitchell

All rights reserved: This book is protected by the copyright laws of the United States of America. No part of this book may be reproduced in any form or by any means, electronic or mechanical, including photocopying, recording, informational storage or retrieval systems, without written permission by the author, except where permitted by law, for the purpose of review, or where otherwise noted.

Published by:
Mitchell Productions, LLC
www.Mitchell-Productions.com

Editing
Stacy Hawkins Adams
www.StacyHawkinsAdams.com

Cover and Interior Design
DHBonner Virtual Solutions, LLC
www.dhbonner.net

ISBN for print version: 978-1-7333754-0-5

Printed in the United States of America

To my mother, Bettye Jean Stanley Mitchell and my sister, Kymelie M. Leonard, thank you for truly being my top fans. Your love and support have always helped to propel me forward in life, business and faith.

Table of Contents

Foreword VII
Introduction IX

Rise to the Occasion 1
    By Althea Simpson

Prospering from the Inside Out 9
    By Eulica Kimber

Speaking Life Over Your Dreams 24
    By Laticia Austin

The Power of Believing 36
    By Dr. Amy Walton

Your "Why" Matters 47
    By Sheryll Golden

Cracking Out of My Shell 53
    By Sandra Hayashi

The Transformation of a Reluctant Leader 62
    By Yolanda Gray

How to Recover from the Storms of Entrepreneurship 73
    By Cynthia Williams-Bey

From Scars to Leadership 84
    By Monica M. Bijoux

Unstoppable 94
    By Pastor Annie Theresa Bryant Fields

Take the LEAP! 102
    By Dr. Marlene Fuller

Building Your Platform 117
    By Sharvette Mitchell

Meet the Authors **129**

Foreword

How you choose to move through the world is up to you. Some tiptoe, while others trot. Some stroll, while others fly. When it comes to business, the rules (and metaphors) you can apply to life are quite the same.

The manner in which you advance in your entrepreneurial or professional career shapes the course of your success; and just as you need business savvy and strategies to thrive, you need motivation and practical advice to shore you up. That, my friend, is exactly what you'll find in *PROPEL*. This anthology was created by social media expert and online strategist Sharvette Michell to help push you forward, into the destiny you've envisioned.

Through inspirational, reflective, transparent and tactical sharing, Sharvette and an impressive list of her personal business coaching clients take time in their personally penned chapters to nudge you forward – past fear, past failure, past false beliefs that you're not ready, good enough or able – into mogul status and a career that soars to the level you desire. If you don't yet have a plan for your future, this book will give you the motivation to sit still or get going, and either way, to start writing the vision.

Once you write it – literally metaphorically – that vision is yours to achieve.

Read each chapter and soak in what it has to offer, in regard to your journey. See yourself scaling proverbial mountains and swimming along exciting shores, because you can.

PROPEL is your roadmap, and Sharvette and her tribe are your steady guides. Congratulations – you are about to win.

~ Stacy Hawkins Adams
Bestselling Author and Anthology Editor

Introduction

In February 2018, after 25 years of faithful service to a major financial services corporation, I walked away from a well-regarded position and a steady paycheck. I leaped head first into full-time entrepreneurship without a huge lottery win, surprise inheritance, or a rich prince of a husband to support me! But let me tell you what I did have... I had faith, a brand, a plan and a mindset.

Typically, entrepreneurs embrace and accept risk. However, I am a person who likes stability. I've had the same phone number since 2001, lived in the same condo for several years, attended the same church since I was 16 years old.... I think you get the point. So how did I wind up striking out on my own? The answer is simple: I am an action taker, and I've learned throughout my life that the earth responds to action takers.

With this knowledge in my hand and heart, I've created a guide – this book, *PROPEL* – to help you and others push aside your fears, your doubts and your reasons why it won't work in favor of achieving your entrepreneurial dreams. This book is not about "how to quit your job," even though that was my story. This book is about how to propel forward in leadership and/or in small business.

Whether you are a leader in your profession, community or church, or if you are building a business from the ground up, there are principles, beliefs, strategies and actions you can glean from this book that will shorten and ease your travel time to your destiny. Isn't that why many of us take a plane or helicopter to a location instead of a car or bus? The capability of the propeller on the plane or helicopter allows you to rise above average modes of travel, gives you a different vantage point and cuts down on time.

Eleven of my entrepreneurial clients and I have joined forces to share our experiences, our proven techniques and the meaningful action steps that helped us propel forward. Each of us has unique backgrounds and experiences from which you'll glean insight and have "aha" moments. Some co-authors have thriving careers, some operate profitable businesses and others are budding into amazing leaders. You will find value in all of the stories and guidance housed in this book collaboration.

I wish you well and I hope you enjoy reading our book. Before you dive in and grow, I'll leave you with this famous Mark Twain quote: "Twenty years from now, you will be more disappointed by the things you didn't do than by the ones you did do. So throw off the bowlines. Sail away from the safe harbor."

~ Sharvette Mitchell

Rise to the Occasion
By Althea Simpson

Which are you afraid of most – failing or succeeding? In my first few years of operating a solo psychotherapy practice, I found myself somewhere in between. It took a ton of intentional and intensive work to "right size" my business and my mindset, which eventually moved me to an authentic place of entrepreneurial success.

What I learned on my path to a thriving business is that fear is an emotion we all experience. Whether rational or irrational, in many instances, the issues that cause us to fear can also paralyze us. It's understandable, then, how entering into entrepreneurship is a decision that can cause tremendous anxiety. As an entrepreneur there is no safety net, and things can constantly change as you try to grow your business. Stepping out of a zone of comfort to pursue your business goals can set you on an emotional roller coaster, where making emotionally-charged decisions leads to lasting ripple effects on your business. Trust me, I know.

The rock bottom I found my entrepreneurial self in during 2015 was a symptom of a childhood that left me craving success and acceptance. I grew up in Southeast Washington, D.C., east of the Anacostia River. In this area of the nation's capital, children were not expected to make it out of their teens. The assumptions were that most of us would wind up dead, strung out on drugs or becoming teenage mothers receiving welfare.

We were counted out, and none of us were expected to achieve society's definition of successful or prosperous – unless you lucked up with some sort of athletic abilities, more specifically football or basketball. Earning a six-figure salary wasn't imaginable for most of the people in my crime and drug-ridden community. However, I knew I wanted something different. I knew the stereotypical path could not be my destiny, and I worked hard to be different, to make something of myself. Yet, even after I succeeded by the world's standards, I was still emotionally bound by the almost daily messages I received as a child – "You are stupid," "You are dumb," "You are worthless."

Long after I had become an adult, those verbal, and sometimes subliminal, beatdowns still ricocheted through my mind. Even with all of my success – an undergraduate degree in business management, a master's degree in marketing, and a master's degree in social work with an emphasis on organizational leadership, as well as experience in business psychology consulting – I continued to pay attention to those negative messages; they seemed to be a part of my DNA.

How did this manifest itself? Although I had beaten the odds, I had a business that I was not running as a business. Operating a business is more than providing a service or selling a product. To be fully effective, it's necessary to have an administrative arm that focuses on business processes and logistics, such as accounting and budgeting; managing consumer orders; strategic planning and human resources management. For the first six years of leading my business, I had none of that in place. My primary focus was to make a living that would allow me to eat and avoid homelessness. No exaggeration – that was my vision.

When I reached the five-year threshold as an entrepreneur, I celebrated my clients and thanked them for being the best part of five years. However, I still didn't see myself as a businesswoman or as a success, especially because a recent attempt to expand had failed.

A year later, I was ready to acknowledge that while I was making money, traveling and speaking, and it seemed like every endeavor I embraced was golden, my business had no substance – kind of like those hollow chocolate Easter bunnies. It looked great on the outside; but I had no processes and systems in place, which in turn, left me unorganized and feeling like a failure. Repeatedly, this refrain ran through my mind: *Why are you beating yourself up? This has turned out how you expected; you're not supposed to be successful anyway.*

I was holding onto the negative messaging that had controlled so much of my life, and in the process, I was playing roulette with my livelihood.

From the very start, I had ignored the need to implement formal processes and got by with just enough clients to make sure company and personal expenses were covered, all the while waiting for the bottom to fall out. Yet consider what happens when you neglect children: It can have devastating effects, including behavioral changes. The same can happen when you neglect your business. Not taking appropriate care of my company and depriving it from much needed nurturance caused some major damage to my finances, including a boatload of tax problems.

That stressful season jolted me into self-reflection. I woke up to the reality that I had to find a way to release the psychological pain that had me feeling less and less confident as a businesswoman before I lost it all. By treating my business as a hobby, I had not been appreciating what it did for me or allowed me to do. I had been so focused on building that I put myself in a financial mess. Money was coming in, but it was going out just as fast.

I had incurred more than $45,000 in debt trying to build my business and secure my future. And then, my emotions started driving my business decisions – so much so that I walked away from a lucrative contract because the stress of my circumstances had triggered my adverse childhood experiences.

Have you ever cried so hard that it felt like you pulled a muscle in your chest? One morning I woke up crying out of disappointment, because the very situation I had tried to avoid was where I found myself close to being – desperate and destitute, like so many in the neighborhood in which I had grown up.

After sitting with this reality for a few days, I finally began to problem solve; and as I sought to repair the business, I knew I also had to repair my sense of self, including my sense of safety and security. I also accepted that I couldn't do this on my own.

Going to therapy put some things into perspective for me. I was able to identify the emotional wounds that still existed and that were blocking my ability to build and sustain a healthy business.

Hurt, fear, shame, guilt and a host of other emotions that I thought had been left in the past were actually showing up as lack of confidence in my business practices.

Therapy also helped me accept that while I had done an awesome job of creating a six-figure company in a five-year period, I had taken the business as far as I could on my own. It was a big step to seek professional guidance and to trust the individuals I chose to help me move forward. So imagine how devastating it was when the first time trying to trust, that failed, too. The business coach and marketing and public relations consultants I hired didn't quite deliver.

I started down the usual path of berating myself, before choosing not to let the negative messages awakened by the setback overtake me. Instead, I acknowledged that selecting the wrong team was just another experience from which I could learn and grow. Sometimes we want to make things happen so badly that we move too quickly and overlook red flags, or even want to give up. I did all of the above.

There were many times when I wanted to quit, but I reminded myself this wasn't an option. I didn't have other people or resources to rely on; living and thriving was all on me. Besides, this was a business I had a passion for and wanted to succeed. Even if this meant fighting through exhaustion on some days and remembering that I liked being my own boss on tougher days.

Once I stopped putting limits on myself and accepted that there was an assignment on my life to help individuals go from "hurt to healed" in their personal lives and in their businesses, I reawakened to the dream, ready to win. I focused my energy on working with clients as both a licensed psychotherapist and as an emotional transformational business strategist, and my company began to soar – this time with a solid foundation.

This doesn't mean that I don't encounter challenges at times; it just means that as I continue to work hard, engage in smart decision making, put strategic business processes in place, and believe in and take care of myself, all is falling into place. What once was only a shell of greatness is now solid, through and through.

While it may seem backwards, change had to start with my mindset before my less-than-stellar business practices could be addressed. After doing the work to move past emotional pain and disappointment, I put a team in place to help me stay focused and hold me accountable to produce the results I desired. My team now includes an accountant, a business attorney and at least one person to handle my administrative tasks. I have been able to clearly redefine business goals and implement practices that have allowed me to create a sustainable and thriving business and a comfortable lifestyle.

What did I learn through all of this? That being strong is acknowledging that you fall weak sometimes, and if at some point you don't fall weak during the journey of starting, building, growing and sustaining your business, then it's quite likely that something is not getting done right. Weakness is not a character flaw, it's character building. Growing and sustaining a business requires more than patience and faith, it requires doing the work.

As an entrepreneur, you are responsible for your business successes and failures. Start celebrating every step and misstep along the way, and don't give up.

If you are already on an entrepreneurial journey or thinking about starting the entrepreneurial journey, here are some of my lessons learned:

1. **Hire a team.** Your business will operate more efficiently and your life will be much more gratifying if you're not doing everything in your business alone. Save some energy to enjoy adult play time.

2. **Develop a supportive network**. Not everyone is blessed to have helpful family and friends. If this is your circumstance, create and cultivate healthy and appropriate business relationships that can turn into supportive friendships.

3. **Write yourself a success letter** that includes and outlines the efforts and opportunities you can control in your business. Here are some examples:

    - Investing Financially and Professional Development
    - Setting Boundaries
    - Implementation

In parting, I encourage you to not let your emotions run your business! Happiness is a decision you make; it should not be based on an emotion you feel. Everyone has positive and negative emotions; embrace all emotions and choose to experience the ones that gives you the most life, light and energy to handle your business well. Give yourself grace when things don't go exactly the way you planned. Since you created the vision, no matter how it turns out, it will be perfect, because it came from you.

I'll leave you with this question to ponder that I hope will propel you to your next level: *What emotional blocks are keeping you from executing in your business?*

Prospering from the Inside Out
By Eulica Kimber

G et paid! Get your coins!
Those are the words we hear every day in our entrepreneurial community, and the Internet has made becoming your own boss a reality for more people than ever before. We are selling courses, coaching, writing and speaking all over the place. But something is missing. As women, we are usually the caretakers of our immediate and extended families. We give of ourselves, pouring, and neglecting ourselves in the process.

I, too, have found myself in the struggle to juggle family and work demands with sprinkles of self-care. This is who we are as women, right? The family CEO who keeps things going, no matter the drama flavor of the day. I once believed this and embraced this role to the fullest. However, nearly a decade ago, when life was good - my husband and I were doing well financially and our young adult daughters were thriving - I was pushed to my emotional, financial and physical limit. My faith was tested in ways that eventually allowed me to discover the value I possess, and to eventually tap into my wealthy place of prospering from the inside out.

During that season, in fall 2011, my husband and I were thriving at our respective jobs, our eldest daughter was in the first semester of her freshman year at North Carolina A&T State University (*Aggie Pride!*) and our baby girl was a freshman in high school. Although retirement was still many years away, hubby and I were excited to take the journey there together. We often talked about the future. Then one day that October, everything drastically changed. My husband, Kevin, went to work that morning at the trucking company he helped manage, not knowing it would be for the last time.

Due to physical and emotional injuries he had sustained during his stint in combat in Desert Storm, he began struggling to walk. Over the next few years, he endured multiple surgeries on his knees and spine, and he also received a diagnosis of severe Post Traumatic Stress Disorder and anxiety.

Not only were his health issues traumatic for all of us, they also became taxing on our well-being, as we suddenly went from a two-income household to me serving as the sole breadwinner. We immediately applied to the Department of Veteran Affairs and the Social Security Administration for benefits; however, we were told that the process could take years (which it did)!

Months after Kevin suddenly fell ill, I spent another sleepless night staring at our bills, praying for guidance. Since I was awake, I decided to get caught up on some volunteer accounting work. As a CPA and professional auditor, I often was tapped to help with the finances of the organizations with which I was affiliated, including serving as treasurer for the PTA at my daughters' schools, and for my sorority and several local churches. As I completed my routine tasks in the wee hours of that morning, I realized I was no longer in a position to share my knowledge and time without being compensated.

God was providing an answer: My skill and passion had tangible monetary value that could meet the financial needs of my family.

I decided then and there to start an accounting business to supplement my income, and putting pen to paper, I outlined everything I would need to launch a successful business. Soon after, I applied for my business license, created a website, purchased business cards and began making connections within the organizations I'd served in the past.

Still, I questioned whether people would actually pay me to do the accounting I had volunteered to do for them for so long. The answer was Yes! And there I found myself, organically building a small business. I began assisting other accountants on audit engagements for churches. I assumed the accounting and payroll for a daycare. I offered training sessions for small business owners and helped them get organized.

I achieved the goal of increasing my family's income, but there was a not-so-good outcome as well: I was exhausted, and perhaps a bit naive. In casting a wide net to secure customers, I had for all intents and purposes become an accounting jack of all trades. There was no focus, no ideal client, no strategic plan for success or growth.

I also made the mistake of setting my rates too low, which attracted less than ideal clients – those whose businesses were not well organized and who did not want to adopt healthy business practices. I believe the reason I did this was twofold. First, I didn't do my homework before setting my rate schedule. Secondly, I really didn't believe that I was worth more. I knew that I should get paid for my services, but I low-balled my prices because I didn't want to scare off customers.

I was worried about rejection, even though I was a Certified Public Accountant with more than 20 years of accounting, audit and corporate tax experience. This perceived inadequacy was compounded by my efforts to seek encouragement and approval from friends and relatives that was met with criticism, gossip and sometimes envy.

I struggled for several years until I met my business coach, Sharvette Mitchell. She was the first person to explicitly state that my prices were too low. My confidence and self-esteem were so low that I was somewhat offended when she made that observation. My mind just could not process it.

I knew then that I had some soul-searching to do. I had to do the work of understanding where my pattern of inadequacy and self-doubt began. I began to notice how I always put myself down and how I could not accept compliments without making an attempt to explain them away, and I realized that I was afraid of success.

I had been trained to agree with the naysayers in my life. I never wanted to shine too much, because I didn't want my family and friends who weren't accomplishing the things I had to see me as gloating. As a result, I never really celebrated my successes. When some in my circle didn't make a big deal about my accounting degree, my great career or even passing the CPA exam, I didn't make a big deal about it, either. It makes me sad when I think about it now, because it's important to celebrate your wins along the way.

My business didn't begin to propel until I learned to prosper from the inside out and disconnect from negative energy. I discovered an author by the name of Brené Brown, a self-proclaimed researcher-storyteller. Reading *The Gifts of Imperfection* and *Daring*

Greatly changed my life by teaching me to accept myself and to see my worth.

Remember, my business was launched from a place of fear! I worried that my family's needs would not be met, and I just wanted to create security. I didn't believe that I should expect more than that, because, I didn't think I was worth more than that.

Eventually, I realized that fear is not a platform from which one should propel. I concluded that if I really wanted to prosper, I needed to ensure that my soul (which includes my mind, will and emotions) was prosperous (3 John 1:2). That meant that I had to only speak words of faith and dismiss the words and actions of some folks. I learned to only share my vision with those who consistently spoke (and still speak) life to me. I had to fire some clients who refused to follow my advice, the law or pay my increased fees, which reflected the value I brought to their businesses. I had to dismiss perfectionism and learn from my mistakes. Finally, I had to look myself in the mirror and say, "I'm good enough!"

Today, you can find several of my favorite Brené Brown quotes in my office. Here are a few:

> "Courage starts with showing up and letting ourselves be seen. Because true belonging only happens when we present our authentic, imperfect selves to the world, our sense of belonging can never be greater than our level of self-acceptance."

> "There is no innovation and creativity without failure. Period."

"Nothing has transformed my life more than realizing that it's a waste of time to evaluate my worthiness by weighing the reaction of the people in the stands."

Over the years, I have built a successful company, Firm Foundation Accounting Solutions, PLLC, and as a result, paid both of my girls' way through college. My husband Kevin's health is stable and we are back in our stride again. I've also shifted the mission of my firm's work to focus on providing business coaching to primarily female entrepreneurs who desire to learn the language of business and make sound decisions based on actual financial results.

You may be thinking that as an accountant I should have started this discussion of propelling into a prosperous business with financial information instead of emotions and self- worth. However, in my experience I've learned that money is one of the most emotional topics there is. Money represents our value in the workplace as well as our years of education and experience. It is the means by which we provide for our family.

Think about one of your worst financial decisions. I suspect that as you think about that decision, you'll recall that it occurred during a very emotional time in your life. The fact is, it's very hard to make sound financial decisions from a place of scarcity and fear.

I like to discuss "prospering from the inside out" with my new business coaching clients. Before we talk about services, sales and expenses; there must be a conversation about your WHY. Why are you in business? Why did you select this product to sell? Why are you targeting this customer?

Taking the time to answer these types of questions will be

valuable down the road as you develop your business model, plan and branding. If your WHY is only about money, you don't have a business; you have a HUSTLE! Hustlers jump from project to project and lack consistency in a persistent search of the next big thing. A business, on the other hand, is paid for delivering consistent value to customers by meeting a need or want. If you have the wrong WHY, at some point you will lose passion for your endeavor and your profits will soon follow.

My most profitable clients are those who are clear about who they are as business owners and who they serve. Clarity makes the next steps of designing the systems and processes of conducting your business easier.

So what is the right WHY? Your why has to be connected to a mission or purpose about which you are passionate. Also, your WHY needs to be connected to a skill or ability that you possess. Finally, your WHY needs to be connected to something you enjoy doing and to people you enjoy serving.

Imagine the misery of being in a business you hate, serving people you dislike! Believe it or not, I run into people all the time who followed the money and not their WHY. They lack the passion and energy to build a sustainable business, and they usually come to me when all has gone wrong.

So now that we've discussed the touchy-feely stuff, we can get to the business of your business. After you have learned how to prosper from the inside out and figured out your business WHY, I want to share with you some principles to keep in mind. I call these principles the "10 things Your Accountant Wishes You Knew." As an emerging woman in business, I want to make sure you understand how to partner with your accountant and fully utilize that person's expertise.

To consistently prosper from the inside out, you must create order and structure around you. Your business won't prosper in chaos. Your business is telling you what it needs, but you won't notice the warning signs of distress if the clues are hiding in piles of paper or a backlog of emails.

This Top 10 list is a great place to start, and your accountant and bank account will thank you.

1. Bookkeeping should take place all year long; not just when the tax return is due. What a terrible time to figure out if you've made a profit or not. You need information from your business on a continuous basis. You are constantly making decisions on purchasing, hiring and customer contracts. You need financial information on a weekly or monthly basis to make course-correcting decisions before you get too far off track. If a customer is not profitable or a vendor is too costly, you need to know that as soon as possible.

2. Don't mix personal and business transactions. You must maintain separate accounts for banking, credit card and other financial accounts for every transaction! It takes accountants a lot of work, frustration and time to sort it all out. As the business owner, you are responsible for reporting complete and accurate information about your business. It is impossible to get a good reading as to where

you are in your business if your personal and business transactions are mixed together. You may think that you are profitable but you're actually propping up your business with your income from your full-time job or another business. I suggest that you have a separate accounting system and a separate bank account for each federal ID number you have registered for the businesses that you've created.

3. Every transaction needs supporting documentation! Remember that your bookkeeper or accountant records transactions to be audit ready at all times. Every income and expense transaction should have a source document, in other words, an invoice, receipt, purchase order, etc. You will find that you may have to go back to a prior year and look at the detail of the transaction. Only the number will be on the financial statement, so you will have to look at the source document to get the details about that transaction. Source documentation is also important if you're undergoing an audit which may be required for a grant or loan application.

4. There is a method to our madness! There are rules and laws that must be followed for recording and reporting income, expenses, payroll, taxes etc. Breaking the rules can cost additional money or jail time and puts your CPA or other license holder at risk of losing their license (which is how we eat) for breaking these rules. I've had clients who tried to get me to pay people under the table, meaning they didn't want to pay employer taxes for them. Other clients have

wanted me to increase income or expenses for a specific outcome in their favor. Your accounting records should be an accurate reflection of the activities of your business.

5. Gross income does not equal profit. You have to plan for and pay your expenses. Many entrepreneurs I've talked to are very focused on their gross income. I'm sure you've heard business owners tout that they have a six-figure business or seven-figure business; neither of which means anything until you see the complete financial picture. For example, if your business grosses $1 million this year, that is a good thing only if your expenses do not exceed that. As you're building your business, pay attention to the entire financial picture. Your business model should produce enough income to cover your expenses, which includes taxes; allow you to invest back into the business; pay yourself a salary AND generate a profit. You may not be able to do that today, but it should be your goal.

6. You can only grow your business through a good accounting system. PERIOD. Data is king! And complete, accurate, timely and reliable data is a powerful tool. With this in mind, please note that Excel is not an accounting system. You need a formal accounting system to properly manage your business operations. There are several web-based programs on the market that allow you to access your information any time and from any computer or mobile device. Wave Accounting, Zero or QuickBooks Online all have similar

access capability.

7. If your accountant is maintaining the accounting records for you, you should have access to the system or receive reports on a weekly and monthly basis. You should also be meeting with the accountant periodically to discuss your financial results and adjustments needed to improve the business. If you maintain your own records, you should set aside this dedicated time to conduct your own reviews on a consistent basis.

8. Your bookkeeping records are only as organized as you are. That receipt stuffed under your car seat will probably not get recorded properly, if at all. Remember, our goal is to prosper from the inside out. Make sure that you are taking care of yourself as a business owner, that is your mind is clear and your goals are documented so you can run the most organized business possible. Systems are important to ensuring that the goals of your business are being met. This is especially true if you have employees working for you.

Processes, policies and procedures should be documented to ensure that your business model is implemented consistently. Customer engagement, recording sales, hiring and paying the bills should follow a set process. When your business is organized, it's easy to train new employees, and your customers receive a consistent and pleasant experience. Furthermore, an organized business will produce complete and accurate financial statements for fact-based decision making.

9. We accounting folks usually charge problem clients more because of extra work involved. Disorganized clients are a headache. I've had to re-key transactions or pour through the statements of multiple bank accounts to figure out which transaction belongs where. This time is much better spent talking about the data found in your financial statements. You're not using your accounting professional to his or her full potential when that accountant is focused on securing receipts and making sure your records are complete. This time will be better spent on refining business plans and making course corrections to your operation.

10. Accountants and bookkeepers add value to your business and want your business to grow! We want to work with you to teach you the language of business. We are excited when you begin to take ownership of the financial outcomes of your business.

I believe that your business is a reflection of its owner. The decisions you make for your business represent your values, priorities and vision. Therefore, it doesn't make sense to create a business with the intent to make money, yet neglect to invest in the tools required to track that money. Organization and investment in this area are vital to the survival of your business.

Investopedia indicates that the most common pitfalls small businesses face are a lack of sufficient capital; poor management; inadequate business planning; and overblown marketing budgets. Additionally, 42 percent of small businesses fail because there's no demand for their services or products. This goes back to my point of your WHY. Are you following your passion to meet the pain point of your clients or following an overplayed formula?

Get clear and comfortable with who you are. You can then find your passion and tap into the wealthy place inside of you.

ASSIGNMENT: Spend some time journaling. This work will take time and space. Dedicate a journal to this soul work. Title it, "My Plan to Prosper."

> *First, look back:* Write about your life, community and work experiences. Describe the people you most enjoyed connecting with. What were they like? How did you support them? What feedback did they give you? Describe the projects that most excited you at your job or in a community organization. What aspects of that experience do you wish you could do every day? How did it make you feel?
>
> *Then look inward:* Who are you? What makes you who you are? Where are you in your journey? What makes you proud? What makes you afraid or ashamed? What experiences and thoughts stop you from seeing the seemingly impossible as possible? Get some tissue and cry it out if needed.
>
> *Finally, look around you*: What systemic problems do you see around that your unique experience, victories and heartbreaks have prepared you to address with joy in your heart? What education, skills and abilities are you equipped with to

serve others? Who and where are the people who have this common need or desire?

From here, start brainstorming your business ideas. Anything that comes to mind, write it in your "Plan to Prosper" journal. Then research your area of interest on Google, Facebook, Twitter, etc. What are people talking or even griping about? What solutions are currently available? How can you address the challenge in your own unique way? Ask questions and create a survey. Become a student of industries relevant to your business ideas.

Follow this process and your business will become a unique reflection of you. Doing your "soul work" will enable you to flow easily into the technical aspects of your business. Your business name and brand colors may come to you from your journaling, brainstorming and researching. There is no need to take someone else's formula and try to fit into his or her box.

You may be thinking, *Eulica, what does all of this have to do with accounting and running my business?* Remember, I started this discussion talking about the way we selflessly pour into others. We give detailed attention to serving our family, job and community. Now, I'm asking you to give that same level of wholehearted attention to yourself and your business. Let your "Plan to Prosper" journal become the place where you envision your business, who you serve and your WHY. In no time, the accounting and administration of your business will fall into place.

When you know who you are and are clear about your journey, your purpose and your value, you will know who you are called to serve and what they need from you.

So, are you now ready to build a successful business? That, my friend, is what I call *Prospering from the Inside Out!*

Speaking Life Over Your Dreams
By Laticia Austin

I became an entrepreneur long before that phrase was common and long before I fully understood what being one meant. As a young adult just a year out of college, I was on a path familiar to me and most of my peers – working for a company that was helping me gain experience and knowledge. Less than six months after being hired, the company began implementing SAP, and consultants worked onsite to help get the software installed.

I got to know several of them during their stay, and they often spoke about what they did for a living and how I could be a great consultant. This world was new to me. Other than growing up in a military family, I wasn't familiar with the concept of being paid to travel and work. So with intrigue, I spoke with one of the consultants I had befriended and shared that I would be interested in learning more.

The consultant asked for my resume, which was a challenge, given that I had only been out of college for about a year and didn't yet have much to share. However, a cousin who was a good writer agreed to help me, and we created my first of many resumes that

I would use to secure clients. I printed the resume, gave it to the consultant and waited.

A week later, I received a call from a recruiter who informed me there was a "project" available for which I was a great fit. I listened to the recruiter's spiel, feeling extremely nervous when she said I would be paid for my flight to and from the project location and given a rental car, hotel and a "daily per diem" for meals. I asked for a window of time to consider the offer and, of course, did what most twenty-somethings do – called my parents. After much conversation and prayer, I accepted the project. I gave my current employer a two-week notice and soon was off to be a consultant. Twenty-plus years later, I'm still at it.

Over the years, the role and legal requirements for professional consultants changed. The law eventually required that I become a business, with a Tax ID and an LLC to continue to operate in the consultant world. In essence, I had to become a small business owner. I must admit, there have been times when I've doubted myself and questioned whether I should just get a "regular job." Each time, my sister would say, "Why?" She was proud of my growth as an entrepreneur and she knew it was my calling.

Before there was an Amazon Kindle or the Nook, I traveled with a book, magazine or newspaper. They were my companions on the plane or when I couldn't sleep at night. While reading, I would notice quotes that I wanted to remember, and I began compiling them in a notebook. I would read the quotes I saved there whenever I doubted myself or my career choice. I still have that notebook, and it has grown into an extensive collection of quotes from others, along with some of my own. I consider that notebook to be my book of affirmations for life.

In today's world, affirmations are everywhere – from vision boards and commercials to Facebook and Instagram, etc. When I started my entrepreneurial journey, there were no social media groups or mastermind circles, or any such thing that I could join for support or encouragement. During that time, there were many rough days that friends and family didn't understand. I would go to the notebook and read the quotes I had written down.

Whether you are on the corporate ladder to success or on the entrepreneurial journey, there will come a time where you will question yourself. Whether it be should you accept the next promotion or attend that conference, or add a new service or product. We don't always have a colleague, friend or family member who understands enough to offer the just-right advice at the just-right time. This is when having an affirmation to repeat can be important.

While there are many existing affirmations you could choose and move forward with, I suggest that every business leader and entrepreneur have his or her own set of affirmations to keep you motivated and focused on the road to success. As a matter of fact, your self-talk is an all-day-long affirmation. You have to realize, though, that what you might be affirming to yourself might not be the best for you. For instance, how often have you said to yourself, "I'm no good at …" or "I might never do …"? These are both affirmations – affirmations that stop you from getting what you want.

Yet, affirmations are meant to help you get over negative thoughts that may undermine your well-being. The practice of positive affirmations and visualization on a daily basis will help fuel your success. Persistence helps you accomplish results much faster than sporadic practice, and practicing your affirmations each day has a positive cumulative effect.

Affirmations by themselves don't guarantee success. You have to take action, but they do provide positive motivation and reinforcement.

> *If your actions inspire others to dream more, learn more, do more and become more, you are a leader.*
> – John Quincy Adams

Here are eight guidelines that are crucial to follow when compiling or creating your affirmations:

1. Be certain about what needs to be affirmed
2. Affirm in the here and now
3. It's all about YOU
4. Engage your emotions
5. Be convinced
6. Be brief and particular
7. Be precise
8. Visualize vividly

BE CERTAIN ABOUT WHAT NEEDS TO BE AFFIRMED

Oftentimes affirmations are created around the symptom of some issue instead of identifying the true cause. If you affirm a symptom instead of the true cause of your issue, you may find yourself accomplishing results in the short term, while long-term results elude you.

For instance, say you think you need a weight-loss affirmation to encourage you to lose 10 pounds. While this might be true – you might need to lose 10 pounds – at a deeper level, the affirmation you might really need is about having a fit, positive body image. While you might, in fact, be heavy, you might also suffer from the notion that your body is ugly, that you're ugly, and so forth. That means you might need two affirmations – one about the loss of weight and one about your notion about yourself. If you merely worked on the affirmation of being 10 pounds lighter, you will in all probability accomplish that result, only to discover a few months later that all the weight is back.

As you start to compose your affirmations, ask yourself, What is my true problem? This might require a good deal of reflection, brainstorming, and honesty.

> *Where there is no vision, the people perish.*
> *– Proverbs 29:18*

AFFIRM IN THE HERE AND NOW

Affirmations are better if stated in the here and now. For instance, "I now have a fantastic job" is a here and now affirmation. "I'm going to have a fantastic job" is affirming something in the future, and even though it's only a subtle shift in the verbiage of the words, your subconscious mind, like a mobile phone, only listens to what you really place in there. Consequently, by affirming, "I'm going to ..." you might well find yourself waiting a really long time for the results to occur because you're forever "going to." Write it as though you've already accomplished it.

This might seem a little silly initially – as your reality is that you aren't a great leader, for instance. But your subconscious mind is far stronger than your conscious brain, and whatever your subconscious mind believes always becomes your reality. If ever you've found yourself saying, "I don't understand why I'm never in a leadership role" it might be that your subconscious has a far stronger picture of your being a non-leader than your conscious has of you being a leader. This technique talks directly to your subconscious mind.

> *A leader is one who knows the way, goes the way and shows the way.* – John Maxwell

IT'S ALL ABOUT YOU!

Your affirmation has to be about you. So, it will always include the word "I" or "me." You can't make affirmations for others. For instance, you couldn't affirm: "My team members are open and honest with one another." This affirmation will never alter their actions. All the same, if you were to state, "I'm open and honest with my team members, as a role model for my team," then you might well discover that your personal change will, curiously enough, have a favorable effect on and lead to shifts in those around you.

Others reading your affirmations might think they sound egotistical and selfish, and that's precisely how they're meant to be, because this is a self-reformation project. Not a "be liked/get other people's approval" project. As a matter of fact, you might do well not to share your affirmations with others, especially if they're likely to put down your efforts or poke fun at you when you don't receive right away what you're affirming.

For instance, say you're affirming, "I'm calm and patient with my children when they're fighting." Then your children are fighting, and you discover yourself screaming at them. Others might laugh at your attempts at changing your actions – "Ah, that affirmation stuff doesn't work very well!" However, they aren't comprehending that these changes don't occur overnight. With persistence and practice, shifts will occur.

> *A man who wants to lead the orchestra must turn his back on the crowd.* – Max Lucado

ENGAGE YOUR EMOTIONS

Emotions provide the power to produce results; i.e., if it doesn't get you charged up, it isn't a powerful enough affirmation. Summon your emotions; be passionate! Adopt phrases such as, "I'm delighted," "I'm so charged up," "It is simple for me," etc. Bring your spirit and your feelings into the affirmation. The stronger the feeling an affirmation brings, the deeper the impression it makes on your brain, and the sooner you experience favorable results.

> *Outstanding leaders go out of their way to boost the self-esteem of their personnel. If people believe in themselves, it's amazing what they can accomplish.*
> – Sam Walton

BE CONVINCED

Make affirmations in favorable terms while avoiding negative statements. Affirm what you do wish, instead of what you do not wish. For instance: "I'm never sad or depressed." What pictures does this damaging statement instantly bring to your mind? Instead, affirm, "I have a favorable and optimistic outlook on life." This statement is much more potent, as it is positive and reinforces your sought-after goal. The words that you choose trigger in your brain emotions and feelings. You want these to be beneficial and uplifting. The fastest and simplest way to ensure that you compose your affirmation in the positive is to identify what it is you don't wish, then ask yourself the question: "What is it that I do wish?" Compose your affirmation from the answer you receive to this question.

> *Become the kind of leader that people would follow voluntarily; even if you had no title or position.*
> – Brian Tracy

BE BRIEF AND PARTICULAR

Brief affirmations are simple to say and have a far greater effect at a subconscious level than those that are long and long-winded. Keeping them specific and to the point adds energy, as the idea is uncluttered by external elements. If need be, have two or three affirmations around the one topic.

> *Effective leadership is not about making speeches or being liked; leadership is defined by results, not attributes.* – Peter Drucker

BE PRECISE

When appropriate, put in numbers what you desire, e.g., the exact weight you wish to be or the precise sum of money you have saved. Or even the individuals that you see yourself being with – e.g. "I am positive and self-assured whenever I'm with John."

> *People buy into the leader before they buy into the vision.*
> *– John Maxwell*

VISUALIZE VIVIDLY

Now that you understand more about your affirmation, the next step to manifesting what you wish for is to vividly visualizing yourself as though you have already obtained it.

> *Leaders must be close enough to relate to others, but far enough ahead to motivate them. – John C. Maxwell*

So today, right now, I want you to create your very own personal affirmations to keep you motivated on your business and entrepreneurial journey. When creating your affirmations, think about the following areas of your life that need affirming: Listening, Being Authentic; Being Transparent; Working Collaboratively; Being Responsive; Being Adaptable; Loving What You Do; Surprise and Delight; and Making Things Easy. This is how you PROPEL.

Make your list of affirmations from a place of positivity. If you are unable to create your own, use the following list as a starting place.

I am a thoughtful person and inspire others with my words.
I am always generous with praise and compliments.
I inspire others to greatness.
I inspire others to reach their goals.
I am an inspiring mentor.
I bring out the best in people.
I have a magnetic personality.
I help others focus on the most positive aspects of themselves.
I help people to be the best that they can be.
I am a born leader.
I lead others by setting a positive example.
I am a visionary.
I know that I can only lead others where I have been before.
I set a positive example for others.
I set trends that others follow.
I lead others by bringing out the best in them.
I remember to thank people often.
I see the world not as it is, but as it can be.
My passion for life inspires others.
With every breath I take, I am bringing more and more charisma into my life.
With every breath I take, I am bringing more and more magnetism into my life.
My story of personal freedom inspires others to seek the same.
My words inspire people all over the world.
Today, I successfully take center stage.
People trust my opinions and expertise.
I communicate clearly what I expect of others.

I take charge easily, no matter what the situation.
People often look to me for advice.
Making important decisions is just what I do.
I quickly engage others in teamwork to optimize results.
People recognize me as a leader.
I am often called on to take charge of a situation.
I embrace responsibility.
I eagerly accept new challenges.
My interpersonal skills are strong.
I am a good decision maker.
People look to me for guidance.
I am able to take the lead.
I am a proven leader.
People always choose me as their team leader.
Leadership comes naturally to me.
I have superior leadership skills.
I make things happen.
I can draw out the best in others

By saying your affirmations aloud each day, or even repeating them silently, your thoughts will move closer to becoming reality. Affirmations move you to succeed by psychologically helping your brain make the transition to what you desire at a more rapid pace. So if your goal is to sell $5,000 worth of product weekly, you may create an affirmation to recite on a daily basis that motivates you to accomplish this feat. An affirmation for this goal could be: "By the end of today, I'll have sold at least $1,000 worth of product."

Utilizing affirmations is an excellent way to help both

up-and-coming and established leaders accomplish their goals and heighten leadership skills. What if you don't believe you're leader material, because you don't possess the skills you believe you need? Begin reciting this affirmation on a daily basis: "I'm a knowledgeable and effective leader." This affirmation should turn your doubt into assurance.

Affirmations ought to be utilized for any situation you would like to alter. Set up a few goals and make affirmations for them. Say them to yourself in the morning, before you begin your day, for best results. You may also say them at different times of the day, as long as you're doing it in repetition. You also can post them in places you'll frequently see them, such as on your bathroom and dresser mirror, your car dashboard, or on a Notes app on your mobile phone. Consider reciting them as well when a behavior, belief, or issue is happening or directly after it's happening. The idea is to say them until you become them.

The ultimate benefit of creating and repeating affirmations is to your health. Studies show that they help boost confidence, lower tension and improve the quality of one's life. So there you have it, leader. It's your time to speak life to yourself, then go and be great!

The Power of Believing
By Dr. Amy Walton

"As a man thinketh in his heart, so is he."
- Proverbs 23:7

During a recent interview that I conducted with a phenomenal female entrepreneur, a singular thought kept running through my mind: *"She believed she could, so she did."*

While many of us are familiar with this popular quote, it resonates with me because it is how I have lived my life and how I intend to approach the remaining years of my life. I want to encourage you to do the same.

Dedication and passion are excellent habits to cultivate; but self-belief is essential for everyone – especially entrepreneurs who want to propel your business forward. The more you believe in yourself and your abilities, the more likely you are to accomplish your goals and reach your dreams.

When I started my first business, I was young – in my 20s – and determined to be professional and successful. I did not have anyone to learn from, but I believed I would figure it out.

I opened my beauty salon approximately a year after giving birth to my youngest son. He was born with a cystic hygroma that covered his face and neck and was attached to some internal organs. He had surgery to remove the tumor at four weeks old, but he continued to have problems tolerating formula. Then, about eight months into his young life, he developed an illness that caused his skin to rapidly sloth off like a snake. Everywhere we went, we left a trail. Doctors didn't have any answers or know of a cure.

At the time, I was working full-time as a cosmetologist in a salon more than an hour away from home. The challenge of balancing work with my family's needs eventually became too much for me, so I decided to take a job outside of this field that would be closer to home. Doing so gave me some of the balance I desperately needed, but I greatly missed doing hair. I would pacify myself by saying, "One day you will."

Sure enough, about a year later, my "one day" came. My youngest son was still having medical challenges and my older son began struggling at school with reading. The stress of trying to meet their needs while juggling everything else escalated, and one morning, while sitting at my desk at work, I decided it wouldn't be for much longer. I would be quitting soon and starting my own business.

I went home that evening and immediately began researching how I could make this happen. First, I wrote out how much I made a week. At the time, I was making $290 a week for a forty-hour work week. Therefore, I determined that I needed to make at least $290 plus expenses for forty hours, and if I could do that, I would be good to go. Next, I began searching for a space to rent that I believed I could afford. I found one for $425 a month, including all utilities. Third, I ordered business cards and purchased used equipment. Lastly, I started sharing the good news with old clients.

Needless to say, about two months later, I gave my two-week notice and began my new venture. I never looked back on what had been; I focused all of my time and energy on the present and on what I was building. I had faith and a plan, and I got started.

Most importantly, I believed in myself. This confidence has made the difference for me time and time again. I didn't need intellect, opportunity or resources – just plain old belief in myself.

As a child, I often dreamt of owning my own salon. In the dreams, I would see the name of the salon and what it would look like. I even dreamt that my husband would be a barber.

When I graduated from high school, I went off to college to pursue my dream of being a doctor. Well, after a few pre-med courses, I realized that was not the path for me. I came home, got a job and entered cosmetology school. I graduated a year later and earned my cosmetology license the same year. Five years later, my childhood dream became my reality: I was the owner of my own salon (And five years prior to that, I married my husband – who isn't a barber, but still cuts it with me).

Luck didn't cut it. Dedication and passion weren't enough. It was believing that I could leave my 9 to 5 job and start a business that helped me do it. It was believing that I could be a boss. It was believing that I could own my own business, even though I lacked role models to guide me. It was believing that God had a plan for me greater than my present condition or my background.

Therefore, when I discover opportunities that are amazing that I don't appear qualified for, I go after them anyway and trust that

I'll figure it out.

> *Live your vision and demand your success.*
> – Steve Maraboli

Here are three effective habits that have consistently helped me increase my belief in myself and shatter self-doubt:

CELEBRATE YOUR VICTORIES

As human beings, we naturally have the tendency to get caught up in our losses and all of the negative things that have transpired, instead of recalling our wins and appreciating all of the good that has occurred.

Many of us are familiar with the biblical story of David and Goliath. Well, David's victory over Goliath is a prime example of what recalling your past victories can do. In 1 Samuel 17, we read that David was a shepherd boy tending sheep who was called by God to defeat a giant that was terrorizing the children of Israel. David was very small compared to the giant, Goliath. Goliath stood about 9 feet and 9 inches tall and was covered in bronze armor from head to toe. But David was not shaken by what he saw. David believed he could defeat the giant. He had a victory mentality. Why? Because David had one thing that Goliath didn't. He had God on his side.

When we have God on our side, we can successfully face any giant. David remembered how the Lord delivered him out of the paw of the lion, and out of the paw of the bear, and he believed that God would once again deliver him – this time out of the hand of this Philistine (1 Samuel 17:37).

Remembering your past victories can propel you forward if you are afraid, stuck or stagnant in your business. In the book of Joshua, the Lord instructed the children of Israel to erect memorials to show their victories. He wanted them to be reminded of His faithfulness and all of the places they had conquered. Maybe you only had one client yesterday; still celebrate that victory.

I remember when I first started my coaching business. I was new to the social media world, so what others had been doing for years on Facebook, Periscope, and Instagram I was just beginning to understand. I had to give myself time to learn and grow. I knew I couldn't compare myself to those who were gurus on social media, because comparison is a killer. I wasn't trying to die before I won.

I had a dream living on the inside of me that was burning to get out, and I wanted to see it to fruition. So, I took what I had learned from the biblical book of Joshua and applied it to my business. I celebrated creating posts, figuring out how to like, share and comment, and showed up every Monday for my Facebook Lives.

I know it may not seem like much, but it was overwhelming to me. I hate to learn new stuff. But what kept me from giving up was celebrating those things that I had accomplished. I wasn't where I started, but I was a few steps up the road. I knew that if I continued to work at it and see myself victorious, I would be just that – victorious.

How many times have you endured difficult situations and arisen victorious? Think about all of those moments in the past, when you thought you would not be able to do it, and you did it. The history test that you passed, the first job interview that you nailed, that deal you closed that was a turnaround for your business...

In moments of self-doubt, let your past victories ignite your faith in yourself and inspire you to thrust forward!

It's a good idea to capture your victories in a journal. This can be victories from yesterday, today, last month or even last year. It doesn't really matter when, but just get in the habit of recording all of your victories. This will bring you a complete sense of joy and accomplishment. In addition, it will reinforce that you are a winner and your success is inevitable. Whether big or small, it does not matter – just celebrate your victories!

GET BACK UP AGAIN

As a female entrepreneur, you will face many challenges, but do not let those challenges stop you. While mistakes and failures are a part of the path to success, do not let those things define you. Those encounters are meant to perfect you.

When I decided to start my life coaching business, I had never created a graphic nor was I technology savvy. This lack of experience terrified me and made me doubt my ability to succeed. It has been a challenge to learn to be confident and understand that imperfection is just learning. Even when the sting of imperfection was still fresh, and the last thing I felt like doing was continuing to build the business, I kept going. In the process, I've gained wisdom from my mistakes, failures and imperfections; and in the bigger picture, those experiences have worked together to build and grow my business into its current state of success.

When you make mistakes, or even fail on your entrepreneurial journey, do not beat yourself. Get back up and try again. The purpose of making mistakes is to learn from them and become better as you propel forward. The time wasted between our failure and trying again is the robber of your days and dreams. Proverbs 24:16 tells us the righteous may fall seven times, but they rise again. This passage of scripture reveals that calamities come upon the righteous, but ultimately, they triumph. Failure, in some instances, is unpreventable. It's your response to failure that matters.

Are you a righteous woman who will get back up? You can, for you are created in the image and likeness of God. God will give you the strength to continue. Again and again you can rise.

The righteous woman takes action. She asks herself the hard questions: *What did I learn? How does this work for me? Who can I help?* This woman continues on the journey that will lead to success, no matter what. She takes what once knocked her down and uses it to propel herself forward.

Beware of the naysayers and the dream killers. They are out there. You might live with them. You might be friends with them. You might even do business with them. They are the type of people who always have an answer for everything. They're quick to give advice from the sideline. They have never actually launched or operated a business. They are people who will poison you with their words of doubt and fear. They will tell you that your dreams are crazy, unrealistic, time consuming, farfetched, unachievable, and on and on. They will nitpick and cause you to lose focus of your goals and stall instead of dreaming for something great with you. They will cause you to abort your dream if you are not careful.

Unfortunately, they are unavoidable. They will find you. So it's vital to know that should you encounter them and they cause you to fall or stall, you must have the courage to get back up again.

Embrace the dream God placed on the inside of you and work it until the day you see the full manifestation of it. Your success will be enviable if you do not quit.

> "Be strong enough to get back up again, even after doubters make you sink to your knees." – Dr Amy

Doubters are everywhere, no matter how pleasant you are or what dream you are chasing. Shut out the noise. The only reason they are talking like that is because they aren't following their dreams and have low self-esteem. Ignore them and believe in yourself until you succeed.

SPEAK UP – TALK LIKE A CHAMPION

We all fall prey to negative talk in life and business from time to time, saying things such as, "I am not the best. Nobody will buy my products. My website is not good enough. I am not tech savvy. I do not take good pictures. I cannot do this. I don't have the resources. I don't have anyone to help me."

I constantly sang that song. I was stuck. I did not know how to get unstuck. I began to do the only thing I knew to do: I sought the Lord. I began to inquire about my lack of success in gaining clients in my coaching business. Back in the day, you passed out business cards and went door to door to get clients. Today, you create a Facebook or Instagram account and work those angles to get clients. I needed to be visible and seen as an expert in the industry. Instead of working to do that I was feeling sorry for myself, entertaining thoughts of not being good enough and incapable of accomplishing this goal.

I knew I was capable, but I did not understand what was hindering me. The Lord spoke and said to me "Your mouth. One day you are speaking life concerning your business and the next day you are speaking death. You have to change your words."

The power of life and death is in the tongue, and those who love it will eat its fruit (Proverbs 18:21). Speak up. Do not speak from the level you are on but from the level you are going to achieve. God demonstrated this power in the book of Genesis. When He created the world, He simply spoke all things into existence (Genesis 1:1-24). You have to do the same if you want to see the success you desire. You have to speak to yourself like a champion.

Champions are people who win repeatedly, and they are held in high regard because of it. Champions change the game! You are a champion. Repeat over and over again to yourself, "I am a champion. There is nothing mediocre about me. Greatness lives within me. Everything I touch prospers." These words are powerful. The words we speak as entrepreneurs will definitely have an impact on our lives and businesses.

I remember in elementary school if my teacher caught you running in the hall she would have you say or write 500 times, "I will not run in the halls." It was torture, but it stopped my classmates and me from running in the halls. Why? First, because the repetition reconditioned our thoughts. Secondly, because we did not like the outcome that running in the halls produced...punishment.

Now, imagine what would happen if you spoke consistently, "I am a millionaire." Eventually, your words would produce millionaire results for you. Trust me, I used to say, "I am broke," and guess what? I was broke!

When I began to change my words, my life began to change. Abundance and prosperity started chasing me down. Opportunities started coming from the left and the right. I have never looked back, only forward, since receiving the revelation to speak up.

When you exchange the negative words with positive life-giving words, the quality of your life and business will began to change. One of the greatest fallacies is that we need to achieve a certain level before we can call ourselves successful. We create our success by the words we speak. God told Joshua to "Keep this Book of the Law always on your lips; meditate on it day and night, so that you may be careful to do everything. Then you will be prosperous and successful." (Joshua 1:8-9)

I encourage you to try speaking to yourself like a champion instead of thinking of yourself as a loser. I guarantee that you will be swept away by the results. It may seem a little strange to speak to yourself at first, but give it a shot and watch the outcome. Talking to yourself like a champion renews your mind. It changes how you see yourself and how you operate your business. When you consistently speak to yourself like a champion, you do not give room to negative and disappointing thoughts filled with doubt, fear, or unbelief. You emphasize with power and conviction, "I am the best at what I do," "There is nothing impossible for me," and "There is nothing average about me. I am a champion."

I leave you with this mandate, which summarizes all that I've shared in this space: You must believe in yourself. Your belief will produce the momentum that will propel you forward. If you fail or make a mistake, understand it is part of the process and take it for what it is....a lesson learned. Do not allow challenges to keep you down. Get back up again. And whatever you desire as an entrepreneur, be sure to speak up about it. Shoot for big targets. Utter words that are in alignment and agreement with your success, for nothing is impossible to you if you believe. Say it with me – "I run a million dollar business" – and let your words, coupled with your belief, propel you forward.

Your "Why" Matters
By Sheryll Golden

Being brought up in a very conservative Protestant church, I wasn't allowed to wear makeup or what were considered "worldly" clothes, such as jeans, shorts or mini-skirts. In my mind, however, the people who were the sharpest wore makeup and worldly clothes – including my cousin Marion, who always looked so sharp at our family gatherings in her red lipstick and jet black hair.

I wasn't the only one who admired Marion; I think most of us did. I suppose part of the reason was her personality. She was friendly, fun and concerned about what was going on in our lives. It was a breath of fresh air being with her because I could laugh, and for a while, not and focus on religion. I was also envious of her ability to live life without following the rules and without fear of repercussions in the afterlife, unlike me. The bottom line, her freedom to live and have fun, along with her confident image, impressed me!

When I became a teenager, my desire to fit in drove me more than my parents' rules, and I began wearing light blue eye shadow and mascara like many of the girls at my school. Makeup made me feel confident and attractive and it felt good to fit in. Then, at age 16, I got "saved," which in the Protestant church means I dedicated my life to Christ. That decision led me back into the conservative existence my parents had modeled and also compelled me to toss the makeup products I deeply enjoyed.

Fast forward about 12 years and I found myself in my late twenties digging deeper into my faith, asking questions about the Bible and the best ways to interpret the Scriptures. When I realized the interpretation I was given in my teens had been taken out of context, I became bitter and angry, knowing I had sacrificed material things I loved. The good that came from it was the realization that I could live freely, like my cousin Marion.

It was as if I had been existing in a fog, and suddenly I became cognizant that my image did in fact matter in how I was perceived by others. I now felt the freedom to venture away from the strict rules I'd been taught and to have fun trying out new makeup and clothes. I grew to a level of grace that allowed me to once again begin using makeup to help me look good and feel more confident.

During this season of awakening, I developed a thirst for more professional knowledge and personal satisfaction. For quite a few years I had worked in a hospital as the secretary of a particular unit where I was responsible for many things, but mostly keeping the unit running smoothly. Secretly, however, I had always wanted to become a Registered Nurse, like my sister and others that I admired in this field. I worked with many top-notch RNs (and doctors); yet, for as many of them as I admired, there were some that left me thinking, "If they can do this, I can too!

I finally summoned enough courage to apply to nursing school. When I was accepted, I was thrilled. While I was waiting for classes to begin, I enrolled part-time in prerequisite classes at a local technical college to begin tiptoeing toward my dream; and as my good grades rolled in, so did a new level of confidence.

While immersing myself in my nursing studies, I accepted an opportunity to become a Mary Kay Cosmetics consultant. Mary Kay taught me a couple of things: the value of good skin care and the best method for choosing makeup for others. It is difficult for me to describe the overwhelming sense of well-being I felt when I began using good skin care products and makeup. I was so immersed in learning more that I was constantly experimenting, yet I felt like I was playing. I was in my happy place, without a doubt.

Where the fun really came in was having one-on-one beauty consultations and taking the before-and-after pictures of my clients. It was exciting to see makeup transform their faces, and as a result, their self-esteem. It felt good to see women become more attractive and confident. I can't say I made a significant amount of money on the Mary Kay venture, but this was my first sense of knowing that I had a passion for skin care and makeup, and I would have done it were there no money involved.

My career as a nurse took the forefront, and the Mary Kay became a social outlet, as I met more people and gained new clients. I realized that in both nursing and my Mary Kay business, I was helping others. Each career provided a way for me to make a difference, which has always been a deep part of who I am.

The training that Mary Kay provided gave me confidence in my own style and methods for wearing makeup, and eventually, I took that experience and to another level. I am now a professional Image Consultant.

This role has been inspired through my knowledge as an RN.

More than most people, I understand the impact healthy skin can have on your health. Couple this with my realization that what matters as much as great skin care and makeup is a positive and professional style (or image). First impressions do indeed matter, and no matter how much people say they are not judging you, they can't help but do so, even if unintentionally. More importantly, most people feel better about themselves when their skin feels good and when they like what they see in the mirror. Great skin provides a beautiful canvas on which to apply makeup.

My journey has led me to the realization that the most important factor in becoming an entrepreneur is to know your "why" – your reason for doing what you do, selling what you sell or sharing what you know. The passion I have for health and beauty makes it easy to share products that are top-notch, quality and healthy, and I love witnessing how changing someone's image for the better can impact their success.

I understand this better than anyone because of what great skin care and makeup did for me. Even I know that when I'm presenting myself in a positive light because I stand taller. The overwhelming sense of self-confidence I've felt when I've received makeovers, makes me want this for others. This has kept me passionate about what I do on my entrepreneurial journey.

Face it: If you go to your doctor and he or she barely gives you the time of day, you know that physician is not passionate about his or her practice or patients. You walk out of the office and search for a new physician. On the other hand, if you go to a doctor who sits down with you or perhaps goes over the allotted time for your appointment, you sense that doctor is really there for you. That is passion. It's as if money were no object, they would still be there for you.

In order to thrive in your business, you have to bring that kind of passion to what you're doing. You can be on every platform available, but if you're not passionate about your work or project or service, people will sense it and be turned off.

So as you venture into the world of entrepreneurship, look deep inside. Ask yourself, *what do I do that comes naturally and feels fun? What takes me to my happy place? If money were no object, what could I keep doing tirelessly?*

Furthermore, as you start looking at what you'd like to do, be willing to take some risks and make some mistakes. I recently read this quote on someone's social media feed: "If you're not making mistakes, you're not trying." It reminded me that even I have been guilty of taking the easy road and playing it safe sometimes, rather than pushing myself and doing the hard work it takes to reach a new level of success. Over the past year, however, I have sought coaching through Sharvette Mitchell that has helped me refine my focus as an image consultant, and I have begun to strategically consider how to become a more visible and vocal leader in my space. In this modern day, I think it's strategic to seek coaching to give you direction. Becoming a leader in your industry sets you apart from other entrepreneurs by giving you an edge.

As an emerging leader, I have stretched myself by taking on some new roles and responsibilities, and I am determined to keep going. Life has taught me that confidence is developed by stepping out of my comfort zone. Just as the baby steps I took to get through nursing school built my confidence, so have my small successes as an entrepreneur given me just the push I needed to move ahead.

Although I don't know where all of this is going to take me, I have enough confidence to get to where I want to be in the moment. I've heard it said that we don't dream big enough, and it's true - sometimes God has bigger plans for us than we can imagine. That's why I'm fine with not knowing whether my dream is complete. I know there's room for more growth, opportunities and success.

As you consider your own dreams, don't limit yourself. Dream as big as your imagination allows. Leave room for bigger things, things that you couldn't have imagined initially. Sometimes when we achieve one dream, it helps us discover more of what God has in store regarding other dreams. Because ultimately, our dreams are birthed through Him.

Cracking Out of My Shell
By Sandra Hayashi

When you are in sales, many think of you as a "Type A" personality – outgoing and able to talk to anyone. However, I have been in sales my entire working life, and I am no Type A.

I started out in retail, where the customers always come to you. There was no pressure to find them. By the time I was 25, I had worked my way up to manager of a CVS Pharmacy in New Jersey. I remained there for six years, until my family moved to Virginia to be closer to family and to seize the opportunity for my husband to own his own pharmacy.

I worked part-time in our pharmacy so that I could focus on raising our children. I also found time to make flags and crafts to sell in the pharmacy and at local craft shows, and made several attempts at selling multi-level marketing products, including Tupperware.

I should have realized that if I couldn't make it selling Tupperware there was no need to keep trying other products, such as magnets and nutritional supplements. There was nothing wrong with the quality of any of the products; the problem was I didn't know how to network. I wasn't comfortable making cold calls, and

I didn't like speaking in front of groups.

None of the companies that pushed these products offered training on how to make connections through networking – only strategies for selling. The concepts of networking and relationship building for direct sales and repeat clients was foreign to me. I was an introvert trying to do business meant for extroverts. Or so I thought.

I have since accepted that you must put yourself in front of the people you want to do business with you. I understand that it's good to provide leads and subtly promote your business while creating a relationship, without the expectation of immediate reward, as it will in the long run provide greater rewards.

In the late 1990's, my husband and I sold our pharmacy, which meant that I needed a new career. Having been in retail for so long, I was ready for something new. I recalled that real estate had always been an interest of mine and decided to work toward a career in that field.

I had taken a few real estate classes in community college before moving to New Jersey and concentrating on retail management, and while living there, my husband and I started exploring the process together. We paused studies when my mother became ill, which was followed by our move to Virginia and a whole new direction.

Now that we were starting over after selling the business, it was the perfect time to return to that interest. However, it still took failing at another sales job – this time buying and selling mortgage notes – before I found the courage to launch my real estate career.

This was in the era before the prevalent use of email, social media and cell phones. The only means of mass marketing were newspaper ads and direct mail. I did this a lot in the beginning, along with using one of the most common marketing tactics of the day – cold calling. This was before Do Not Call legislation was passed, and I (along with others in sales) would go through a list or the phone book and try to drum up business.

I was never very good at this, as I always got tongue tied while trying to get through my prepared speech. I never had a problem talking to people who called in or walked into the office seeking information. I knew these people were looking for what I had to offer, so it was much easier to connect with them.

Several years later, my first attempt at networking opened up a new world for me. A new broker in the real estate office for which I worked encouraged me to join a group called the Women's Council of REALTORS®. During these times there was a great divide in the REALTOR® community between those "North of the River" and "South of the River." I was a Southside girl and very nervous about going to The Country Club of Virginia to meet with all of these ladies from "North of the River." Thankfully, my fears were unwarranted. They were nice and polite, and several even encouraged me to consider membership. However, I felt out of place and had no idea how to fit in; so after one or two meetings, I stopped going.

In 2011, I joined a networking group of men and women in different industries. Everyone would share their profession and services and refer business to each other. Everyone was super nice, but still, that never felt right.

I occasionally attended other events throughout the area, but If I was alone, it was always the same – wandering around, hoping someone would talk to me or that I would see someone I knew. It was always uncomfortable. Yet, I didn't give up, and today, I can share some of the practices I finally adopted to make networking more effective.

They include:

- Regular attendance. My lack of confidence kept me from consistently showing up, which kept me from forming relationships.
- Taking the time to get to know the other members on a more personal level. Had I done so, I would have grown more comfortable in asking questions and sharing information about my business.
- Putting more effort into presenting myself as someone they would want to do business with, by sharing how I would be a great choice for them to recommend to others. Instead, I thought, "Hey, I'm here, making my quick speech of who I am and what I do, now you should work with me." I found out it takes a little more effort than that.

There are many more examples I could share; and in part, because networking didn't come naturally, I hit a very low point in my career. While I kept my real estate license, I did very little for about 18 months, choosing to concentrate instead on another business I operated – serving as mobile notary public. This role required short interactions with one-time customers who sought out my services. It was what I needed to get over feelings of failure.   A few years later, I found the courage to try real estate again, and eventually connected with a loan officer (Alison) who invited me to attend a meeting of a group she belonged to – the Women's Council of REALTORS®! I shared my experience with her from years ago, but she encouraged me to try it anyway.

I attended a meeting in May 2015 and was amazed by how comfortable I felt this time around. It was a larger group. People floated about, talking and laughing; I knew people there. I wasn't a fly on the wall. People walked up to me and made me feel welcome. After the meeting, I decided to become a member.

Around this same time, I decided to partner with a different real estate agency, a choice that also pushed me out of my comfort zone and into new territory. I now worked from home without office support staff. I was now responsible for all of my advertising and lead generation, and I couldn't just walk into my broker's office and ask for advice. It was sink or swim time, and I was determined to swim.

Then, an acquaintance named Shanna K., who I knew from the Women's Council, invited me to attend the meeting for a new group she was starting called FABWomen. Finally, my eyes were opened to the fact that networking can be fun. You don't have to stand around in a stuffy room, talking in quiet voices, passing business cards to people who will throw them away when they get home. The Women's Council and FABWomen, and the people in them, helped turn my life around. After meeting her at a FABWomen presentation, I signed up for a class given by business coach Mary Foley called "Power Up Your Presentation." I wanted to be able to give better presentations to my clients. Little did I know, that class would come in handy for so much more.

Some of the REALTORS® at my new firm were also Women's

Council members and had gotten me involved by inviting me to serve on the membership committee as a greeter. My job was to find the people standing alone and make them feel welcome, making sure they weren't hugging the corner the way I had done so many times. This was my first real test at proving that networking didn't have to be scary.

I would go into those meetings each month seeking out the "wall flowers." I would introduce myself, ask a few questions about who they worked for, how long they had been in business and then introduce them to someone else in the room.

These are easy questions to ask when you are talking to someone for the first time. It's a way to find common interest. Once you ask the question, STOP and LISTEN to the answer. Paying attention to the person you are talking to and not scanning the room for whoever else might be around is a sign of respect. Another important point of etiquette is to wait for people to ask for your business card (unless you are in a group where they are being passed around); and when they give you theirs, take the time to look at it and make a comment before you just stick it in your pocket.

By late summer 2016, I had begun to feel comfortable in both Women's Council and FABWomen meetings, and I was even looking forward to attending. What a change from 2012 and 2013, when I almost completely cut myself off from interacting with anyone but the few real estate clients I had and the clients from my notary public business. I was approached by members of the nominating committee of Women's Council and asked to be the Treasurer for the next year. I easily said yes, because it was low profile and I have always been pretty good with the accounting side of business. Well, about a week later, I get a call asking if instead of serving as Treasurer if I would agree to serve as President-Elect. To say I was shocked would be an understatement; but with some gentle nudging and encouragement, I said yes.

My year as President-Elect was easy. I wasn't expected to put myself out there, but I did make it a point to get to the meeting early and talk to as many people as possible. I felt like I was in the shadow of a very popular President, so, I watched her lead from a distance, and luckily had the support of other members of the group to show me the path to what I could expect when I took the helm. What I learned from this experience is that you must surround yourself with the right kind of people – those who will support you and encourage you to be your best self.

When I began my term as President, I also assessed where I was in my business and what improvements I needed to make. One important step was to enroll in a group program to help "Rev Up" your business with Mary Foley, who started me on the path to being able to say yes to the opportunity to be President.

I learned many things while participating in this group, the most important being what I stated earlier: You must make the right kind of friends and business associates — those who will offer symbiotic relationships; connections that will look out for you and your business the way you will for them. For example, when you are at meetings together talking to people and you find someone that your friend should meet, introduce them! Plan before you go who you want to meet and what you want to get out of a meeting, then share that with your friend so you can help each other.

Another practice I've adopted to keep in touch with some of

my REALTOR® friends is to share upcoming events and continuing education classes with them and ask them to join me. It's a great way to stay in touch with people I don't see very often and makes for better working relationships.

When you meet people at an event who you think would be good business advocates or who you would enjoy working with, follow up with them. Send them an email letting them know that it was a pleasure to meet them and that you would like to include them in your network. If they are local, invite them out for coffee or lunch to further explore the opportunities for working together.

Don't have time for coffee with a bunch of people? See if they have time for an "AIR" conversation. This is when you ask if they have a little time to talk by phone to give you some Advice, Insights and Recommendations. Be prepared to ask them a few questions about something you have going on, then listen to what they have to say. It is good practice to restate some of what they have said so they know you are getting their point; and tell them how much you appreciate them taking the time to talk with you and give you their opinion. This can be used with people you have just met, with past clients or with people you want to reconnect with after a long period of time.

My year as President went well. I became comfortable in front of the room leading the meetings because I had a great program director who put together quality programs for us to present to the members. This year, I assumed the role of program director, and these responsibilities have nudged me to put myself out there even more than in the past.

Just four short years ago, I never would have been able to contact local and sometimes national speakers and confidently work with them to plan programs that regularly fill the room. You must show up and become involved in the groups or organizations that work for you. Volunteer to be on a committee or become an officer, if that is the structure of the group. This is how you build your confidence and increase your recognition with a greater number of people.

Through connections made at events, you must choose to be with people that nurture both your mind and your soul. The people that have come into my life have shown me how to grow personally and professionally. Having gone for years being closed off from much of the outside world, just working inside a small circle of acquaintances, I now understand that you must go out and find the right people to have in your life, not just those with proximity.

My insights and ability to be comfortable in most networking situations comes from the programs I have attended over the last several years. The local and national Women's Council meetings, as well as FABWomen, and the guidance of Mary Foley and Sharvette Mitchell, have been amazing resources for me.

It is important to seize appropriate opportunities, learn from others, and give help to those you can. You can't live in a bubble and expect to know and do it all yourself. Making the decision to change your life is not easy; it looks different for each one of us. The journey is ongoing and will take many twists and turns as you try to find what works for you. It all begins with you.

Good luck!

The Transformation of a Reluctant Leader
By Yolanda Gray

I've never been one to seek the limelight and I've never been accused of being one of those "natural-born leaders." In fact, I've always done my best to maintain a low profile, by ducking out of the way when a search for leaders of any kind was underway. Since childhood, I've known how to "disappear" into a corner and become invisible.

Not that I would have to be concerned about leading anyone or anything. I couldn't even secure the honor of serving as line leader in kindergarten – a job I desired because only then I would know that my teacher approved of me.

Being raised in a home that demanded my silent obedience, leaving me unable to speak up for myself, kept me locked up inside myself. The words spoken to me while growing up molded the belief that I wasn't capable of doing anything right. I didn't understand until many years after childhood that this environment wasn't conducive for the process of becoming, which meant that instead of feeling confident and bold, I cowered and doubted myself. The true essence of a leader is the ability to influence others to follow.

Why would I ever feel "in charge" or able to boldly, confidently lead others?

During the early years of my career, I manifested this belief about myself by staying in the background and securing jobs as the top assistant to the top leaders in the corporate and public sector. This offered me a place to shine, but not too brilliantly. I was satisfied knowing that my bosses approved of my abilities to get the job done and make them look good.

In these executive-level positions, I eventually grew comfortable enough to assume small leadership roles, on committees and projects. One year, when I served as executive assistant to the warden of a California prison, the March of Dimes asked the city's administrators to participate as a town-wide team for the organization's annual walk and fundraiser. My boss agreed to do it, and he selected me to spearhead the entire venture! His vision was to create an impact in the local region that would wow the town and his superiors in City Hall.

From team T-shirts to soliciting donations, I undertook a larger-than-me assignment. There was no way to crawl in a corner, under a desk or say, "Give this to someone else more qualified." The part of me that sought approval of others – at this juncture, my boss – wouldn't allow for this response. I made a decision to step up to the task.

Using my strategizing and organizational skills as the Warden's executive assistant, I sat down and listed every detail that would have to be managed to achieve our goals, which were to make lots of money for the March of Dimes and make the city look good doing it!

I was excited and terrified at the same time. It was so important to my boss that our facility represent the town in the most positive light, and I wanted to make that happen for all concerned. I also knew this one thing: I was not going to pull this off by myself. My boss had given me carte blanche to get the job done, so I enlisted assistance from all my resources, including the inmates, through their print shop supervisor.

Engaging others to join me on the mission wasn't difficult because of an already established rapport through my professional interactions with the supervisors of the inmates and the leaders and employees of our facility. The inmates took great pride in designing and printing the town's logo on about 200 T-shirts. They made signs with the town's name on them for the mile markers, and they even collected money to donate for the babies who would be served by the March of Dimes' programs. The mayor and the city council offered their support. Everyone in town got in on the action.

On the day of the walk, it was wonderful to see our team wearing our fancy T-shirts and walking past the mile markers created by the inmates. There was a party-like atmosphere. We had balloons, food and drinks, and the families of the officers and City Hall staff and community members also participated in the walk and in the fun.

As the event unfolded, an overwhelming sense of pride and gratitude filled me. I had actually stepped up to a leadership role and taken responsibility, instead of hiding in the corner or saying, 'Get someone else to do that part and I'll help.'

I realized that had my boss not put me in charge, I would have missed out on the resulting success. I also realized how much I enjoyed watching someone's vision come to pass. Getting on board with another's vision was the beginning of my revelation about my calling as an influencer, organizer, and motivator. Being a part of something larger than my world inspired me to keep going, even with all of the challenges and long hours connected to a big project.

I could not have done this without the established connections and relationships in my workplace. I knew I could request and receive help, which I have found to be the most important value in leadership. Asking for help from those you have respected professionally and positive working relationships create the environment for getting the assistance you need to complete a major task.

We led our team to a powerful finish that day. At the awards ceremony, our town received the highest award, for the most money collected. The little town of 4,000 beat out neighboring towns seven times bigger! My boss received kudos from the Mayor and the City Council. There was a proclamation issued at the next City Council meeting in recognition of our efforts. I had become a leader – a reluctant leader, but still a leader.

Now, this big victory didn't motivate me to want to replicate that leadership experience. It was great that we were so successful, but I didn't begin to consider the next big thing. I was still content to be the right-hand person of the leader so, I continued to play small.

Opportunities continued to present themselves; but in my mind, I never believed I was a leader. I was given another big project – organizing and facilitating the state prison's annual compliance audit. Again, I rallied my resources. Those who had participated in the walk stepped up and made sure their respective departments were in order. We all wanted the report to reflect the warden's and the city's excellence. It wasn't just about me; it was about all of us.

What I didn't realize at the time was that I was developing my strength as a leader. Even for one with natural leadership skills, the gift must be honed. One has to train and practice to become successful, then replicate the next time and the next time. I was unknowingly in training.

Several years later, my boss came to me with another great opportunity that took me straight out of my comfort zone and dropped me into a minefield of tests, challenges and emotional upheaval. It meant moving from the known to the unknown, including relocation and leaving behind of my family and friends.

That year, at age 43, I left my position as the warden's administrative assistant and began a new career in another state prison. It was an exciting, but stressful adjustment. I was about to learn the power of influence, the challenges and responsibility of leadership, and the fulfillment of a job well done. But first, my inner strength would be tested.

To prepare for my new role, I lived in a paramilitary environment for six weeks. During this time I had to trade my high heels, suits and lipstick for a drab uniform, bulky boots and no makeup. The worst part was the isolation from family and friends. We operated in a tight structure and took marching orders from harsh, unrelenting commanders. We underlings were tested every day – emotionally, physically and mentally.

I was up at 4:30 a.m. every day, heading over to the gym, the track or wherever maneuvers were happening. After physical training, we'd go back to the dorm to shower and get dressed, making sure our boots were spit-shined, clothes pressed. Make-up and nail polish were forbidden. It was tough to maintain a feminine appearance.

During one of my days off, I found a hair stylist to cut my shoulder length hair and style it into a pixie. If your hair wasn't up and off the shoulders, you were in violation. So, I sacrificed the long, pretty hair. With the early morning wake-ups and drills in the middle of the night, there was no time for managing it.

After physical training (known as P.T.), we would head over to the chow line before the drills and begin classroom lessons. A typical day ended at 8 or 9 p.m., and the next day was just like the day before. I had never lived such an existence. The grueling discipline to maintain the schedule and achieve the expected high standards fully tested me. But then it happened again: I became a reluctant leader one more time.

I was chosen by my sergeant as squad leader of a company (platoon), and life inside the compound took on a whole new dimension. Now, I was responsible for more than just myself. I had to make sure that the recruits in my squad were up and at attention for inspection at roll call. I didn't want to be the one charting the course! I didn't know how to do this work! My biggest worry was that I wouldn't gain the squad's respect and be able to motivate them to action.

A good leader seeks assistance from others who effectively lead. I sought out the squad leaders within my company and asked them to teach me how to do this job. They were younger than me and had been in the armed forces, so they were accustomed to the regimen.

These young men spent many hours teaching me how to march in cadence, how to call out commands, the call signs on the radio, and so much more. I also found the one mature man in our company who was leading a squad. I went to him with all of the questions I had about how to do this job, and about its expectations and challenges.

Then I engaged my squad members. I had already established connections with most of them, hanging out with them at chow, during breaks; being a part of the team. They trusted and liked me.

Most importantly, I felt respected by them. I was one of the oldest women in the academy; some of them turned to me as a confidante. It made me determined to give them the best experience by leading by example. I worked harder than I would have had I only been responsible for my actions and outcomes. Classroom studies were rigorous and challenging, so we all would study together late into the night; and when one of us passed our exams, we all passed!

I truly cared for all of the men and women in my squad and enjoyed praying for them and encouraging them. Some of them were desperate to succeed. I know I was. I had left everything behind to take on this new life. Encouragement and support kept us going.

I set the tone for the day (shiny boots), pushing hard during physical training. I won first place for the fastest female runner because my entire company came out to cheer me on all around the course! Did I mention already that I was one of the oldest women in the academy? We all came together as a strong, solid unit and went on to win first prize for the best company in the entire academy!

Had I not been recruited, selected, forced – whatever word

comes to mind – into a leadership position, I am sure I would not have volunteered. Like the young girl I had been in school, I diligently sought to be the one behind the scenes, invisible and serving to make others shine.

I realized that fear had kept me from saying, "Here I am, send me." It had kept me safe. I couldn't fail if I didn't step out; and I avoided rejection by staying in the shadows of the "real" leaders." Stepping up to the challenge, seeking help, caring about the outcomes for all and being one amongst the many taught me about true leadership, and I learned some things along the way.

The first was that **leaders are not always "born."** I believe in destiny. The Bible is full of stories of reluctant leaders; but when it's your turn, you will obey or you will shrink from the responsibility and miss out on the excitement of watching a big project unfold and people elevated to their rightful place. You may also miss your destiny, and the destiny of others to rise and shine in their calling.

Second, **leading is influencing**, which means getting others to go along with the plan and working together to make sure it happens. You can't lead if you can't influence others to follow you. None of the two major events I orchestrated could have happened without others buying in and agreeing to do what was necessary.

Third, **influence only comes by connecting with others BEFORE you need them.** This doesn't mean operating in a manipulative manner. I always seek an authentic connection with others. Being relatable and interested in the other person is how I am wired, and I saw how crucial it was when it came time to ask for support.

Fourth, **leaders must tap into their resources**, knowing where to go for the right tools and the right people with the strengths that are relevant to the plan you're trying to execute.

Fifth, **it's not about the leader.** It's all about the people you lead and the mission you're focused on honoring. The people who worked with me to create a successful March of Dimes Walk for the city in which we lived probably would have done it anyway because it was the warden's project. However, it wouldn't have had the same magnitude of impact on our entire town had there not been complete buy-in.

Sixth, **a leader rises up and develops other leaders.** Both the warden and my sergeant empowered me to do a big job. As leaders, they had faith and confidence in my abilities. If they believed I could, then I had to believe I could. I will forever be grateful to these two men and the others who have given me the opportunity to lead when I thought I was incapable.

Empowering others to lead is how Jesus made extraordinary disciples of ordinary men. What a shining example of lifting others up to go out and do what He taught them. He said they would do even greater things than He!

Today, I believe I was in the right place at the right time all along. The pain of my childhood and upbringing could have left me forever in the corner, feeling invisible and being ineffective. Had I not embraced the vision others had for me, stepped up and sought help from those around me, I would not be doing work that I'm currently loving.

I believe in destiny, and because someone saw something in me that I couldn't see in myself, I am forever grateful. Some years after I left corrections, I wanted to create a fun, refreshing and power-filled women's retreat. I gathered some women together to get behind my vision and they helped me successfully execute it.

I only led that retreat for two years, but it continues under new leaders. The number of women attending has increased in the decade since its inception, and the rotating leadership every year or two gives others a chance to rise up and lead the vision. Today, my role is to facilitate the workshops and assist in any way I can. I can be part of and revel in the amazing moments of the weekend.

As a life coach, I now lead a community of women who want to walk authentically, powerfully and confidently in their purpose. As these women pursue God's promised higher life, I help them chart their course by connecting with them at a deep level, in every session. They become empowered leaders of their own lives.

I have watched in amazement how the power of believing in someone completely transforms a life – both on my own journey and through the lives of the women I serve. God changes lives and circumstances; He leads me and then I lead others.

As a speaker, I work to influence change by sharing my story of overcoming adversity, alcoholism and lack of self-worth. The message is always this: You can exchange your life for the one God designed for you. You don't have to stay stuck in a past of negative, false, and limiting beliefs. You aren't what happened to you. You are destined to lead in some way. Your messy life can become your message, and you can become a leader of change. Showing others your transformed self is leadership by example!

At the events and gatherings I host for women, nobody leaves feeling left out or hopeless. They know I care. They learn to care about themselves. It's not about me; it's about showing them a different perspective and mindset. This selfless, mission-minded focus is probably the most important quality of a true leader, and I'm grateful to have developed it over time, in the right time and season.

How to Recover from the Storms of Entrepreneurship
By Cynthia Williams-Bey

This chapter is dedicated to my husband and partner Andri Williams Bey; my six beautiful children – Joshua, Lyric, Madison, Andrea my angel in heaven (RIP), Mackenzie and Elissa Stohrm; my sister and personal editor Lavonia; my team – Kia, Cynthia, Stephanie, Michelle, Teasia, Tanya, Carolyn, Trakia, and Beverly at Heaven Sent; my family; my friends; my Pastors, Jay and Ashley Patrick of Liberation Church, and to all of my supporters who have been with me and encouraged me through the storms.

When I opened a child daycare center more than 14 years ago, I had no idea what it took to run a business. It was literally a step of faith that I took as an act of obedience. The best way to describe what my experience was like is to ask you to envision the work of a solider. In the business world, the marketplace is the battlefield and entrepreneurship is the war being fought. I saw it that way, because while it can be worthwhile and quite rewarding, entrepreneurship is not a path to be taken lightly or approached by those who are afraid of challenges, which sometimes can feel like storms.

When it comes to entrepreneurship, you have to know how to maneuver around pitfalls and survive in unfavorable elements. There are some things that can only be learned on the battlefield; and the frequency and depth of your storm will vary, based on where and what you are building. However, if you can handle the challenges and storms with courage, focus and faith, you can not only survive, but also come out wiser, stronger and better equipped to operate your business from a place of both passion and mission-driven focus. I've learned these truths through firsthand experience, and what I've come away with are a set of steps that can help you get your bearings and keep going:

- Dry Off
- Assess the Damage
- Identify Areas to Strengthen
- Salvage the Debris
- Redraw Your Blueprint and Rebuild
- Stay Prepared

DRY OFF

When we get caught in the rain of a natural storm, our human nature is to take off our wet clothes and dry off. However, as an entrepreneur, we often do the exact opposite when storms arise. We want to dig in our heels or run for cover or pretend that we're not even wet. This approach not only can impact our business, it also can impact us personally.

My advice? Take some time to take care of you. In doing so, you'll be better able to take care of your business.

I learned this firsthand in 2017 when I faced a crisis in my business that wound up affecting my health so drastically that I suffered the loss of the child I was carrying, in my first trimester of pregnancy. During that time, an audit, unstable staff and unexpected allegations regarding my business practices left me scrambling to fix things to the point of neglecting myself. My stress levels were so high that neither my body, nor my baby, could endure, and for the second time, I lost an unborn child.

Yet, the entrepreneur in me wouldn't quit. Within 24 hours of my miscarriage, I went back to my office – on pain medication, still bruised and emotional, yet determined to save my reputation and my company. Now, some may say that's dedication and perseverance; but on the opposite end that can be a dangerous space for someone to be in. Yes, during that period I had to do what was needed to save my business; however, this should not be the norm. For me, it was the norm to deal with a personal crisis and still be at the office working. After a while, this can take an emotional toll on anyone. Your business is not worth your mental and physical well-being. I honestly should have been relaxing and dealing with the loss of my child. The office should have been the last place on my mind or in my schedule.

Not drying off after a storm can lead to several problems, and that's exactly what happened to me. Prior to me losing my second baby in 2017, I pushed myself to the limit, which caused me to have to step back from operating my daycare for a few months and go on bedrest. There had been no time to prepare someone to effectively fill my role, and in the absence of my hands-on leadership, everything fell apart.

I had tons of parent complaints, unpaid invoices, disgruntled staff. That few months of absence caused a whirlwind of storms for me upon my return. There were so many complaints that my state's licensing agency stepped in and reduced my ability to operate to a conditional license.

I'm confident that much of this turmoil could have been avoided had I paced myself better and took time to make decisions from a position of being well-rested and operating with a clear focus. Instead, by trying to act first and singlehandedly keep things afloat, I was not alert enough to notice things that were out of alignment.

Secondly, when you choose to keep going (or not "dry off" after a storm), you risk the well-being of your family. In my case, my first miscarriage in 2013 not only affected me, it also affected my entire family, and many of the kids at my daycare. Everyone was excited and awaiting the baby's arrival. The second time I lost my baby, many didn't know I was pregnant and I was relieved, because I just don't know how I could have handled the questions and aftermath like I did the first time around.

Lastly, refusing to pause and "dry off" puts you at risk of making things worse. When you are not focused and tired and weary, you can possibly create a whirlwind of other storms that could have been prevented if you were healthy with a clear mind.

So, before you try to go in and fix things after you've been hit with trials and issues that arise from running a business, take a moment to make sure that you are good first. Once you have absorbed the situation and have had a moment to breathe and gather yourself, then you can dive in with a clear focus and graceful strategy to face your challenges, both professionally and personally.

ASSESS THE DAMAGE

Now that you have had some time to dry off after your business storm and regain your strength, it's time to assess the damage. This is a critical step to ensure that you identify the areas of your foundation that did not hold up. During this time, you are not trying to fix anything. Your main focus is to understand what didn't work.

Review your policies and procedures. Are they clear and concise? Do they include steps or actions you will take in the event of a particular crisis or challenge? Are both your staff and clients aware of these policies and procedures? What systems do you have in place to ensure that both staff and clients know and understand your policies and procedures?

In my daycare center, for example, it is policy that all children who enter the facility be checked for communicable diseases as well as bruises. If a child enters our facility and there is a bruise discovered, we immediately document it and question the parent before the child is left in our care. If bruises are not visible, my staff does a second check when they change diapers, etc., and there is a second teacher on hand to witness the second check. If a bruise or other questionable mark is found, it is documented by both parties, and the parent is contacted immediately.

The policies and procedures that you put in place can either protect you from a storm or make you succumb to it. If a client were to decide that he or she was not satisfied with your services and wanted to form an allegation against you, what guidelines or policies do you have in place to protect you? With appropriate policies in place, it will be harder for someone to make false accusations that hold merit.

IDENTIFY AREAS TO STRENGTHEN

Now that you've identified the damage, you can focus on the repair. An important part of this process is to identify and acknowledge your business's weak points. When thinking about weak points in a foundation, think about your business' structure and organization. Even though it's good to assess this from your role as the visionary, it's always best that you start with yourself. You are your business' greatest asset, so if your weak, then everything else will follow suit.

In my case, when I took a moment in 2017 to consider how my business would operate if I had to step back, I realized that it couldn't function well. I saw that I was my business's biggest weakness, because I structured everything around myself. I handled payroll, I handled human resources, I handled transportation and so forth. I had fallen into one of the biggest mistakes you can make as an entrepreneur – trying to manage everything.

I wound up meeting with a business colleague (Tosha Frye), who showed me a method that would save me so much time and effort and allow my business to run more efficiently. I was able to figure out what I should do as the owner, what I could delegate that would require follow up, and what I could allocate without following up. Based on my team structure at that time and their overall strengths and abilities, this is an example of what my list looked liked:

- Things only I could do as the owner included payroll, paying taxes, setting up contracts, establishing partnerships and making major financial decisions.

- Things I could delegate but had to follow up on included lesson plans, parent clock-ins, student assessments, child records, collection of tuition payments, meal counts, parent tours and new registrations.
- Things I was able to delegate without having to follow up on included purchasing gas for vehicles, grocery shopping for the center and making copies.

Delegating these tasks saved me so much time and energy and allowed me to focus on critical areas. Even though it was hard to release some responsibility to others, it freed me to accomplish more and strategically focus on the business.

It serves neither you nor your business if you are still needing to turn around and do tasks that your essential staff should be handling. And while we are speaking of it, ensure that you have clear job descriptions for your staff so that you don't receive any push back when you are implementing this new system.

So I want you to take a moment and think about the things you can take off of your plate as the owner. Once you complete this list it is important that you now take these tasks and split them up amongst your staff according to job descriptions, strengths and weaknesses. You want to make sure that the people you are giving these tasks to are well equipped to handle them and to do so professionally and excellently. If not, you will continue to face challenges.

Throughout this process, be sure to identify your business' strengths, so you can build upon them. Compare the strongest areas of your foundation to the weakest areas to determine what you can transfer over to make the entire foundation stronger.

SALVAGE THE DEBRIS

How many times after a storm or trial in life have you seen people throw out the damaged debris? If there is anything I can tell you, it's that the debris is the most important remnant of the storm. If you look closely, you can find wisdom, knowledge and even instruction in the debris. Debris will tell you how and what parts not to build with next time and also reveal what decisions and actions led you to the current state. Debris will tell you what soil is good and rich. Debris will tell you your story.

Many of us tend to get rid of the debris, because it reminds us of the lessons and heartaches we've had to deal with. Yes - the debris tells us and shows us our weaknesses; it tells us and reminds us of our failures. But how else are we to grow and mature as visionaries?

Major debris in my business journey accumulated in 2015, after I opened my second daycare center. I was excited, and the staff and parents were excited; but it turns out that I wasn't as prepared for the growth as I believed.

When I had to shift focus from the first location to get the second one off the ground, the directors of my first location became overwhelmed. They were not fully prepared to handle the tasks of overseeing daily operations alone. Secondly, the first center now had to carry the financial burden of the new facility until enrollment increased. This caused a huge issue and led to me being unable to make payroll. I had great staff, but not being paid on time can affect the morale of even the most dedicated. We were just not ready as a team or a business as a whole to sustain both locations.

So only a few short months after opening the second location, while eight months pregnant, I was forced to close my first location. My entire staff, except for one person, resigned.

I was humiliated, hurt and felt like a failure. That experience has stuck with me ever since, and I've used it through the years to remind me of the choices that led me to that position. I have been able to use it for improvements as well. I was able to bring some of the systems I had from my first location that worked very well over to help my second center run better, so that I would never be in that situation again.

I am proof that there are some lessons that stick with you, that cause you to push yourself and to make sure you cross as many I's and dot as many T's as you can, going forward. The debris from that storm in my life allowed me to identify what I could handle. Even though the circumstances were not favorable, I was able to see my strength under pressure. I was able to understand how much of a blow I could take without bowing.

When I face storms today, I always have the debris of my first facility shutdown to encourage me and remind me that I've dealt with worse situations. The memories allow me to have peace while encouraging and strengthening me for the next battle. I ask you, where is your debris? Examine it and use it for good.

REDRAW YOUR BLUE PRINT AND REBUILD

To effectively recover from a storm, you must take in everything and begin to sketch out a new vision. Draw out a plan with the new structures. Keep everything that held up during the storm, and replace every weak point with a stronger policy, procedure, employee, etc. During this process, make sure that everything in your foundation is completely thought out. It's also a good time to perhaps compare the strong parts of your foundation with the weak parts to see if you can perhaps use the same steps you used to build that particular part with the one you are repeating.

It's also good to bring in a second set of eyes or a selected team to take a second look at your business structure, policies and procedures to determine if there are any missing links. It would be wise for the second set of eyes to be offered by a person or a team that has nothing to do with your daily operations, in order to provide an unbiased opinion.

Sometimes it takes someone from the outside to determine whether your business and its systems are weak or strong. When I went through my rebuilding process, I sat down with one of my daycare center parents who happened to be my sister in Christ, as well as another sister of ours, who had no association with the daycare. They were able to share insights about areas they considered strong, weak, in need of improvement, etc.

After sitting with them, I started to include my staff in my new process of hiring and I also implemented new and higher standards to weed out some of the applicants. As a result, my staff turnover rate decreased dramatically, and my parent complaints went from every other week to one or two a month, and eventually to one every six to twelve months.

I even saw a change with the children's behavior. Children that had been coming to my office on a daily basis were no longer coming and were able to be redirected by the teacher in their classes. Most importantly, my bottom line increased, because communication with parents was clearer and expectations were set regarding payments and registering children through the state system for proper payment, etc.

When drawing your blue print, you want to take your time. You do not want to rush this process. You want to start from the lightest parts of the organization to the heaviest - meaning you don't want to start from the top but from the bottom, entry level point.

Before you start any project, you want to have some basic components in place. Take a moment to answer the following questions so you can begin to map out your blueprint:

- Do you have client contracts?
- Do you have employee and client handbooks featuring your current policies and procedures?
- Do you have non-compete and nondisclosure agreements?
- Do you have clear job descriptions?
- Do you have lines of authority and an organizational chart that's clear to both clients and staff?

AND FINALLY...GET PREPARED AND STAY PREPARED

The best way to prepare for your next storm is to use elements from the last storm. You often grow from your mistakes and use those lessons to do better next time around. So, when you are faced with an obstacle during your journey, keep these instructions with you, to help you survive and thrive.

From Scars to Leadership
By Monica M. Bijoux

It is often debated whether leadership is something you are born with or something you can learn. I personally have found that my life experiences, especially my trauma, have shaped my leadership abilities in ways that now allow me to fully serve others.

From my perspective, leadership is the ability to successfully guide someone to a desired destination. It is not just about being the boss or being in charge. True leadership is about knowing people, knowing when to lead or follow, and knowing how to help your team grow while meeting deadlines, completing goals and having positive outcomes, despite difficult workplace situations.

People often believe that in order to be a truly good leader, a college degree is necessary. However, I know firsthand how life experiences can give one the wisdom, skills and resilience required to handle significant responsibilities and to effectively make decisions. Although I now have a college education, my first leadership position occurred when I was a twenty-year-old high school dropout with a GED. When I gave birth to my daughter at the age of seventeen, I was not allowed to finish high school, so I snuck out of the house when my mother left for work and completed courses at the local community college to obtain my high school diploma. Soon after, I started dispatching for a multi-million-dollar ambulance company that also ran calls for 9-1-1. Within a year, I was promoted to serve as the first female supervisor for the company.

I did not know the impact of my leadership style until five years later, when my mother was having a heart attack. She contacted 9-1-1, and based on where she lived and not having insurance, she was being taken to the nearest hospital, which was a county hospital. When the ambulance arrived, one of the paramedics recognized my mother's last name being the same as mine and asked her if she knew me. My mother informed the paramedic that she was my mother. The paramedic told the other paramedic (and my mother), "She is not going to County, she is going to the Loma Linda, because [Monica] was the best supervisor I ever had." My mother told me later that Loma Linda is the number one hospital for cardiology in California, and because of my leadership skills, I saved her life.

The scars from my personal trauma and experience as a teenage mother played a key role in my leadership abilities. Everyone experiences and reacts to trauma differently. In my case, it has served as fuel for my healing; and while on this journey, it has allowed me to pour the wisdom, discipline, tenacity and focus that I used to succeed into those around me – in particular those I lead at work.

I was sexually abused as a child, and as a result, my senses are heightened, enabling me to easily identify when something isn't quite right. Instead of using this keen awareness to mistrust others, as so many of those exposed to trauma do, I use it to become more discerning about the behaviors and needs of my colleagues and staff, and I can sense when something is going on in their lives. Paying attention to others and being sensitive to their needs has shown those I lead that I am there for them. Being there for others not only includes paying attention and acknowledging their wins, but also being aware of when there are challenges, and stepping in to assist as necessary.

After undertaking the intensive work required to heal, including therapy, I made the decision to use my abuse as a springboard for growth. Doing so has helped me ensure that my team at work feels nurtured and empowered, and that boundaries are put in place and honored to prevent abuse from occurring there. Boundary setting is an essential asset for leaders to possess. Leaders with clear boundaries are leaders who are less stressed.

I have been told I am the queen of boundaries, because I am always clear with those around me about what I will and will not do, tolerate or expose myself to. I set boundaries for who I spend time with, what I put energy into, and how I spend my time. Boundaries are not something you place on others; they are instead a form of protection of you and others.

In a work environment, boundaries prevent favoritism, enable consistency and maintain fairness. Consistency and fairness create an environment of trust, and that trust creates an environment of peace, which further prevents an environment plagued with abuse. Boundaries also allow employees to feel safe, as they know what to expect and know their limitations.

I learned how to set boundaries after giving birth to my daughter. I was determined not to expose her to the kind of abuse I had endured growing up, and the only way I knew to protect her was to put parameters in place. When I spent time with my daughter, I spent time only with her and prevented interruptions from others. I was only a teenager; however, I knew I had to prioritize what was important and, in that season, it was my daughter.

I have carried this thinking into my leadership roles. Employees feel valued and appreciated when you take time to listen to them. So remember, setting boundaries is not a bad thing.

The ability to communicate, or the lack thereof, impacts your effectiveness as a leader. Being able to clearly express what is needed and being fearless in expressing it makes for a well-informed team or unit. A good communication style consists of being clear, concise and consistent. Having these three elements leave little room for confusion. Communication also breeds competency, confidence and teamwork. When I was a dispatch supervisor, a female district director told me, "'When you walk out of a room and someone can fill your shoes, then you are truly doing your job as a leader." This was the best advice I have received as a leader.

Don't be afraid to keep your team informed of what is going on in the company. One of the biggest complaints I have heard from employees of companies I have worked for is the flow of communication being nonexistent.

I once heard the story of three sponges of different sizes; small, medium and large. The large sponge gets wet to the point it is full; however, it just sits in the water and eventually grows mold. The middle sponge gets wet and its excess water is squeezed into the smaller sponge; so now the middle sponge is able to absorb more water. The medium and small sponges are able to absorb and hold more water than the big sponge, due to sharing.

Let's equate the use of water with leaders' practice of sharing information. Suppose a leader receives information and doesn't share it with anyone. After a while, that leader will be so overwhelmed with details and facts that confusion sets it on what to do and whom to ask for help. Alternatively, had the leader shared the wealth of information, the team could have worked together to brainstorm ideas and/or solutions.

Another key component of good leadership is feedback. Feedback is two-way communication and should not be used solely for correcting others' behavior. Feedback allows leaders to discover what their teams believe they are doing right and receive feedback on potential adjustments that could be helpful. I have always told those I lead, "I have your back; however, I will always hold you accountable." I let it be known from the beginning my expectations and ensure I provide constant feedback along the way.

Every employee I've led has told me how much my style of giving and receiving feedback has made a difference for them, because they each felt supported from the beginning. Feedback should not only be provided before, during or after an appraisal, it can be conducted any time, even just to say "good job."

I use feedback as a tool to learn what type of leader each employee needs me to be in order to excel. I also ask what things I can assist with in order to help them reach their goals.

No employee is the same, and you cannot supervise or lead each employee the same, because someone will feel left out or lost in the shuffle. Providing honest feedback while also being open to receiving honest feedback only enhances department morale and builds on your goal of open and transparent communication.

Another important leadership skill to possess is the ability to lead from the middle. I've often heard leaders say they lead from the front or from the rear; however, leading from the front makes it difficult to see behind you. Leading from the rear, allows the leader to see only those immediately in front of her. I have found that leading from the middle allows the leader to see everything, the employees to feel supported and other colleagues to feel as if you are approachable.

The ability to see and focus on the entire team provides inclusivity and reduces feelings of favoritism. It is easy to go to the person you see every day instead of the person who is right for the job. Some of the best employees are introverts and spend more time avoiding the crowd or being seen. Leading from the middle affords you the opportunity to see everyone and to include the introvert.

I personally am a person who prefers to work behind the scenes; however, I am often pulled to the front to complete a job because I have had leaders who led from the middle and noticed my abilities. I didn't have to shine a spotlight on myself, and some of your best employees won't either.

Leading from the middle involves getting from behind your desk and routinely speaking to your team and asking how they are doing. You will be able to see, hear and get a good sense of office morale for yourself, rather than based on what others say. When your team sees you, they should not feel as if they are in trouble because that is the only time they see you or hear from you.

Additionally, leading from the middle allows the leader to form a more cohesive bond with her team. You will come off as less intimidating, more approachable and more invested in your people, instead of just focusing on whether a task is completed or whether you've improved the bottom line.

While you are doing your walk-about and getting to know your team, you have the opportunity to acknowledge each individual's hard work and dedication. This will help each member feel accepted, validated, acknowledged and respected.

Growing up, I endured a lot of emotional abuse, which included being ridiculed because of my intelligence. This caused me to focus on what I considered to be negative things about myself, and hanging around abusive people stunted my emotional growth. At age 15, I received an opportunity to attend a college preparatory high school where I was surrounded by highly intelligent students. Being around like-minded peers, I came out of my shell and was able to be my authentic self. I found my voice and began to emotionally heal and develop mentally. This experience taught me that even though I was different from others in my biological family, there was an environment where I fit – one that nurtured me and helped me to accept myself for who I am.

Years later, the life lessons I learned in both my unhealthy and healthy environments have served me well as a leader. Not having my successes, accomplishments and abilities acknowledged or celebrated for years, I made it a point to ensure that those I led did not have the same experience. Being around like-minded individuals afforded me the opportunity to become the person I wanted to be; therefore, whenever I lead, I try to ensure that others feel respected, validated or acknowledged.

Being around like-minded people and those with the same goals and ambitions has also helped my growth and development.

As a leader, growing and developing yourself is important, as you can't give what you don't possess. A great leader is constantly working on personal and professional development. As a leader, it is important to surround yourself around people who inspire, motivate, and push you to grow, develop, and elevate.

Another quality of good leadership is the ability to mentor others. A mentor teaches with humility, dignity and honesty, not with an air of arrogance or selfishness. As a leader, you may not know all of the answers; however, connecting an employee with someone who can help him or her grow and develop is priceless. The additional knowledge received not only benefits that employee, but the entire team.

Mentors are also important to acquire. I had teachers, my mother's friends and my peers' mothers mentor me through my childhood trauma, I seek to pour into others what they poured into me. They gave me hope, increased my confidence and helped me believe I really could do anything. I want everyone I lead to leave my presence feeling the same – especially those that I mentor in specific ways or for specific purposes.

Another characteristic of great leadership is the ability to hear and the willingness to listen. Growing up, I was misunderstood and never felt heard. The phrase "Children should be seen and not heard" was repeated often and routinely through my childhood. It is for this reason that I make it a point to listen with the intent to understand.

I also don't walk into a leadership role immediately ready to make changes. Instead, I observe, ask questions and get a history of why a particular process has been adopted in order to determine if change is necessary. When changes are warranted, I talk to the team about my recommendation while receiving input from those who will be executing the changes. This helps the team feel heard and knows that their opinions matter. This also helps you with buy-in. Resistance to change occurs less often when there is inclusivity in the process.

Finally, transparency is a must for a great leader. Having a leader who is transparent is like having a golden ticket to the Willy Wonka Factory. Transparency breathes vulnerability, humility, humanity and trust.

Being open and honest about who you are helps employees get to know who you truly are and what makes you tick. Unfortunately, you did not come with a label that says, "Handle with care and wash at 300 F." No, transparency is not about partying with your employees, dating any of them or telling your business. It is about being honest about what you feel, think and believe about a situation. It is about being open and vulnerable versus secretive.

Creating a secretive work environment causes anxiety for employees and promotes stress in the workplace. A lot of leaders keep things secret because they feel that those who know what they know are capable of taking their jobs; but if an environment of transparency is created, it eliminates the need for competition and allows everyone to help everyone, which also lessens the stress. As I stated earlier, when a leader walks out of a room and another person can fill her shoes, that leader has done an excellent job.

Allowing my trials, traumas and tribulations to be a catalyst for greatness has helped me create a workplace haven of empowerment, growth and genuine happiness; and employees aren't the only beneficiaries. I am, too. As Maya Angelou once said: "People will forget what you said, people will forget what you did, but people will never forget how you made them feel."

Unstoppable

By Pastor Annie Theresa Bryant Fields

I could smell the heavy scent of alcohol on his breath as he pressed the gun into my rib cage. I distinctly remember the cold feeling of the barrel of the weapon against my flesh, and my entire body shivered. I felt fearful and angry all at the same time as I prepared to die.

My life began to swiftly flash before my eyes, and I even saw my first husband, my son and my daughter. The next thing I knew, I had taken my eyes off the gun and looked the gunman right in his eyes. I began to boldly pray these words out loud:

> "Father God in the Name of Jesus, if this is my last day on earth, I ask you to forgive me for any and every sin I may have committed today and wash me in the Blood of Jesus, whereas there is no spot or blemish in my soul... Please make me whole, so I can look at your Son, and my Savior Jesus, face-to-face and hear the words to enter in Your presence! And Lord, please take care of my husband and my children. Let their lives be filled with blessings, joy and

peace! Take care of my entire family and all my friends and let them remember me as a vessel filled with Life and Love!

And God, PLEEEASE don't let this moment be in vain. I ask you to save and deliver this man and save his family and everyone connected to him. Don't let him walk this earth in bondage, filled with sin. Forgive him and let him be a vessel to share your Word with others. And I pray that he will NEVER do anything like this to anyone else ever again.

I ask you in Jesus' Mighty Name! Amen."

While I prayed and continued to look him dead in his eyes, he jumped back off of me with an unexplainable force. This man was 6 feet 2 inches tall and weighed more than 270 pounds, but he literally backed off of me as if someone had lifted him up and thrown him back.

He grew extremely nervous and began pacing fiercely while waving the gun. I wasn't sure what was going to happen next; all I knew, from that very moment and whether I lived or died, was that I was UNSTOPPABLE!!! I was assured that my walk and relationship with Jesus Christ would enable me to conquer anything I may face in life. My life Scripture, Philippians 4:13, resonated loudly in my spirit: "I can do all things through Christ which strengthens me."

Since that life-altering experience, which happened more than 25 years ago, my mantra has been to not let anything or anyone stop me from pursuing any goal, dream or wish I may have. As a leader, three elements which always remind me of this affirmation are:

- To consistently forgive others when they offend, hurt or betray me.
- To keep a positive mindset during any challenge, adversity or obstacle I may face.
- And, to persevere with passion, regardless of what life may bring.

Wikipedia describes forgiveness as "the intentional and voluntary process by which a victim undergoes a change in feelings and attitude regarding an offense and lets go of negative emotions, such as vengefulness." This is how one moves forward, rather than staying stuck in the past.

In life and business, conflicts occur. However, powerful leaders recognize the need to forgive and to help others forgive someone who has offended or disappointed them. One of the most courageous acts of leadership is to relinquish the temptation to take revenge on those who oppose your views, thoughts and/or decisions made as the leader for the good of the group or the health of the organization.

I honestly believe forgiveness is medicine for you (not just a gift to the person who offended you), because it directly impacts you and every aspect of your life. As an educator, pastor and entrepreneur, there have been many instances in which those under my leadership and I have agreed to disagree; but when it came down to making sound decisions, they felt hurt, rejected and resentful. Afterwards, I would receive the cold shoulder and be excluded from social occasions, special events and projects in which I had previously been included. On many days, I felt like it was them versus me.

Nevertheless, it was extremely important to promote forgiveness. I would acknowledge the harm or injustice which may have been experienced by others while reminding everyone of the vision and mission of the organization. Furthermore, I would demonstrate deep regret for the conflict which had taken place while encouraging everyone to use the experience as a restoration tool to move forward.

Restoring trust and self-worth has always been more important to me than exerting leadership power. One of my spiritual leaders always used to say, "It's important to make the wrong right, even when you're not in the wrong." I wholeheartedly agree with him and make every effort to bring peace to any situation. This doesn't mean I waver from the sound professional decisions I must make as a leader; instead, I seek to make sure that others feel they are valued, regardless of any disagreement that may occur.

Mahatma Ghandi once said, "Keep your thoughts positive, because your thoughts become your words. Keep your words positive, because your words become your behavior. Keep your behavior positive, because your behavior becomes your habits. Keep your habits positive, because your habits become your values. Keep your values positive, because your values become your destiny." This quote has been a profound roadmap for my entire life. In addition to making sure I forgive others quickly and immediately, as I did with the gunman who accosted me, it has always been extremely important for me to keep a positive mindset about everything and everyone I encounter. American philosopher William James said, if you "believe that life is worth living, then your belief will help create the fact."

Sometimes maintaining a positive presence at your business, job, ministry, or even your family organization, is much easier said than done. However, by being mindful of your own presentation and making a conscious effort to exude positive energy, you can make an immense impact on your employees and the overall culture of the company. People remember how you make them feel, and they are going to react to whatever energy the leader permeates. "As a man thinketh, so is he" (Proverbs 23:7). Powerful leaders set the tone of their organizations, and displaying a positive attitude is a key element for effective leadership.

As an entrepreneur, I have found many times that leaders can set the tone of the culture of the company by the way they present themselves to their team. If leaders want a positive environment in their organizations, they must do whatever is necessary to provide that culture. One of the paths to positive thinking, and one of the by-products of positive leadership, is self-awareness.

A study conducted by Leading Teams found that managers have the greatest influence on whether an office environment is positive. According to the findings, 54 percent of employees indicated this was the case.

This makes sense, because leaders who have a great outlook on life are usually looking for the silver lining in any situation, they experience greater joy in life, and they are always resourceful. Positive leaders know their circumstances can be improved. They foresee a better future and pursue it wholeheartedly. They embrace challenges, knowing that something important will be learned. In every step taken, even when some are backward, positive leaders see a benefit. They are confident that diligent effort pays off, and they persevere in storms because they know there is sunshine on the other side.

Perseverance is another key ingredient for shaping successful leaders. Blend perseverance with passion and you'll reap optimal rewards, notes Angela Duckworth, in her book Grit: The Power of Passion and Perseverance. Many people have significant skills, talent and knowledge, but they do not persevere. Leaders who are passionate about their work, and about supporting and guiding those under their charge, are driven to stay the course, day in and day out. These leaders want to continuously improve and develop a skill until they've mastered it. They learn to withstand defeats because giving up is unacceptable to them. Circumstances may change, but a purpose-driven leader's calling doesn't.

C.S. Lewis once said, "Hardships often prepare ordinary people for an extraordinary destiny." With this in mind, during devastating periods of my life, I have acquired a No Excuses, No Regrets mantra. I constantly remind myself and other leaders to eliminate excuses; and when you are passionate about your work, this is indeed possible. If not, making excuses can become an embedded part of who you are and compromise your vision and effectiveness as a leader.

As a cancer conqueror (not a victim), I'm determined to show others that stopping or giving is unacceptable. Even during my worst days healthwise, I press to work, to serve in my ministry, and to run my business passionately and consistently. When others tell me I don't look like what I'm going through, it's because they see me working diligently, even if they have just witnessed me intaking chemo or experiencing nausea at its highest form. My call to lead gives me strength to endure, and to do so with grace and joy. When leaders are passionate about what they do, this is truly possible.

Many times as I reflect back on that beautiful spring day 25 years ago when my life hung in the balance, I wonder if things would have been different if I had allowed fear to consume me, instead of believing and trusting in God, and trusting in who I was to Him. Could the fear I experienced for that brief moment have cost me my life? Or, would I have survived the experience yet been fearful of challenges and adversities for the rest of my life? Would I have given up whenever threatened by others, believing that I wasn't good enough or big enough to accomplish greater things? Would I have pursued dreams which were unusual and unheard of, despite what others thought? Would I have had the strength to pick myself up and move forward quicker, better and with an even more positive attitude after falling several times within these past 25 years?

I'm forever grateful for having a personal relationship with Christ that was solid enough to the point that I could forgive the gunman in the moment of him robbing me and pray for his salvation. In that moment, on that day, my leadership in Christ reached new heights.

It was powerful to realize that I could remain positive, knowing it could be my last day on earth, and to realize that I could boldly look the perpetrator in his eyes and see a distraught soul who needed to know God. When the gunman allowed me to go into my house (being that the incident occurred only a few feet from my front door) and I was given a chance to celebrate the 7th birthday of my daughter (who, by the way, was looking out of her bedroom window but didn't think anything was wrong because all she heard was what her mother normally did – praying for another soul), I knew I had more purpose to fulfill.

I identified the gunman in a lineup, and he was prosecuted and served time. Several years after the incident, I did some inquiring and learned that upon his release from prison, he had received Jesus Christ as his personal savior! He is currently a manager with a great company and is a leader in his own right, in his church's ministry. God used that young man to teach me to be unstoppable as a leader, and He used me to help that young man discover the greatness within himself. That's what good leaders do – give, receive, and give again. That's what can make any of us who lead with forgiveness, positivity and perseverance UNSTOPPABLE!

Take the LEAP!
By Dr. Marlene Fuller

> *"Success is liking yourself, liking what you do,
> and liking how you do it."*
>
> —Maya Angelou

When my son was seven years old, he asked me one day while we were shopping about buying a needless toy, just as he had done on so many other occasions. Instead of catering to his request that day, I told him that I could not buy him everything he wanted, and if he wanted things that he did not need, he must earn money to buy them.

With child-like faith and passionate courage, he immediately began looking for a job! He didn't discuss it with me – I discovered his attempts to find work when he began speaking to store clerks about completing job applications. He was disappointed when each store told him that he was too young.

Soon, he began talking about starting a business because of the closed doors he had encountered. It took him two years to develop an idea that was "mommy-approved." (I am ashamed to admit that most of his constraints during that 24-month period occurred because I was the naysayer to his dreams, finding fault with every product idea.)

Just before he turned ten, however, and with the encouragement of his grandmother, he launched a business making custom greeting cards. Within six months, he expanded his business to making silver bracelets.

I helped him as an initial financial investor and operations lead. Yes, he gave me a job with very little pay. I was ecstatic to see his vision come to fruition and watch the buds of entrepreneurship blossom. No matter what he encountered, he was determined to take the leap towards his dream of being a kid-entrepreneur and having the freedom to manage his finances. Fast forward to today, and his dream has blossomed him into a dynamic leader who is more independent and courageous than I ever was at age ten.

Each of us has a longing to strive for something higher; to go to places about which we initially can only dream. This may be a hope or a dream for our professional lives, the start of a business, the livelihood of our families, our health, finances and so much more. In the moment of dreaming, we have a choice to execute action or to live only with the fantasy.

One of the things I learned from the experience with my son is that I had a fear of failure. After more than twenty years of working in corporate banking, I was afraid to explore the unknown, even if there was a dream. If I tried and it did not work, then that would be my greatest pain. But my son's greatest fear was that he would not be able to initiate his business at all. He was willing to learn. He was willing to fall down. For him, failure is never having a chance to even try.

This chapter is for the courageous and the fearful who desire to take action and fulfill your dreams. Here are ten tips to help you reach your goal, assess if you are stuck, and experience the joy in leaping.

#1 Have A Vision for The End Before You Begin

Creating a vision begins with the dream that awakened the passion in your soul to do something. A vision helps direct your steps. This is the GPS for where you are going. You may not know all of the tasks to complete, but you have a vision for what the end product or service should be. Consider what it would be like to move into your dream home. Before you can speak to a realtor or the building architect, you must have a vision for what you want to build. Apply the same principle to your targeted career or business ideas. What is your vision?

In the end, I will build or accomplish:

_____
_____
_____
_____
_____
_____
_____
_____

#2 Take the LEAP on the Right Set of Stairs

Each set of stairs is a path to your goal. Make sure the path you have chosen is the right path. It is crushing to climb several flights of stairs and discover that the stairs are not headed in the needed direction. In my journey, I have lost momentum because I was on the wrong set of stairs. I thought this was a sign that I had the wrong goal and I should abort my efforts. However, when I gave up on my mission, the dream and the passion never went away. This meant that aborting the mission was not the right solution; I just wasn't on the right set of stairs.

Gather advice from trusted business leaders, professionals and even those who took the leap and failed. Your constraints may exist because you lack skills or haven't exerted enough effort. It may be the wrong path to accomplish your goal. Or, it may be the wrong time to execute. Each resource will provide valuable lessons (good and bad) to help you discern the path that you should travel, and when.

Who can help you to explore the path that you should take? Try to identify at least three people and ask them for referrals of others who guided them. Then begin to build an execution plan to implement.

List at least three people you will contact this month to offer you guidance:

_____
_____
_____

#3 Assess Uncomfortable Signals

If you have never done a particular thing before, expect that you will be uncomfortable. Being uncomfortable doesn't mean that something is wrong. It does provide a signal for you to assess what you're doing, how you're feeling, and whether you are progressing. When I was most uncomfortable, it required that I utilize secondary skills. I needed to think and operate in a way that I was not accustomed.

As a project manager, I like having a plan and managing tasks tightly. I am most uncomfortable when there are no defined tasks and the team does not collaborate. In these challenges, I become creative in building relationships in a short period of time and leveraging the relationships to drive the results. As an introvert and multi-vocational career woman, this burns tremendous personal energy, but the results are worth it. In the chaos of my discomfort, I strengthen secondary skills in relationship building and experience the joy that comes from hurdling difficult obstacles and winning!

What makes you uncomfortable? What skills do you have that could help you drive success that you normally do not use?

_____
_____
_____
_____
_____
_____

#4 Dare to be Unique

My son developed business ideas when other kids his age were not thinking about owning a business. Daring to do something may mean that you may be the trendsetter. And just because you are doing it, doesn't mean that others have to join you. Dare to be unique, validate the market need and go for it!

Now, if someone does have a similar business idea, spend some time exploring how you may establish a competitive advantage over your competitor. In my son's case, there were no other kid greeting card businesses in the area, and even when he began making jewelry, there were no other kid entrepreneurs in the area who made silver jewelry.

If you are not an entrepreneur, this approach still applies. Employers look for differentiating skills and competencies to hire new talent and offer promotions. Colleges and universities look for exceptional leadership skills and academic performance. Embrace your unique qualities and strive to be the best.

What competitive advantage do you have or can build over your competitor?

_____

_____

_____

_____

_____

_____

#5 Enjoy the Journey, Not Just the Destination

Each round of the journey to your dream will take you higher and higher. But what good is reaching the dream if you would have missed the excitement of learning something, meeting new people, celebrating milestones and having fun along the way? A focus on enjoying the journey will keep you from retreating back to the old landing step. This focus will help you to avoid poor leadership behaviors, because you will experience joy in growing and watching your dream unfold.

I had to learn how to enjoy falling down in order to enjoy my journey. Some of my greatest moments have resulted from the lessons I learned after falling and standing up again. For so many years, I worked hard to avoid failure, relaxing only after I reached my goal. Even then, I didn't spend enough time celebrating the accomplishment because I was already planning the next effort.

However, I've come to realize that what gives my heart life is experiencing a full life with my son. It became important to experience the highs and lows of the journey with him, because it made the journey more enjoyable for me and instilled drive and tenacity in him. If I waited until the end to simply celebrate the journey with him, we would have missed so much along the way. The light that gives my heart joy is knowing that I am fulfilling God's will – both for myself and in raising my son.

As a pastor, this has sustained my faith and helped me experience the joy in loving others, especially the ones who didn't love me in return or made it difficult for me to love them. Follow the light that gives your heart joy.

Take a moment to reflect on what gives your heart light. Then create a simple plan to experience more of it!

_____
_____
_____
_____
_____
_____
_____
_____
_____
_____

#6 Seek Exposure and Visibility

In my corporate experience, I have the option of working from home. As an introvert who is multi-vocational, I enjoy the work-from-home days without having people walk by, wanting to engage in small talk. However, when I work from home, I lose exposure and visibility, which is critical for taking leaps forward. We need exposure and visibility with the right people, and exposure to the heart of the business, in order to offer dynamic and timely solutions.

Connections are vital to our brand. When I began to make myself more available for exposure and visibility, I also began to build a network of advocates who could speak to my skills and accomplishments. Having advocates will expand your reach to other leaders, especially when you are not in the room.

Where can you seek additional exposure and visibility? Do you have advocates that are helping promote your brand? Write a few steps you can take to cultivate these relationships.

_____
_____
_____
_____
_____
_____
_____
_____
_____

#7 Embrace Risks

Not only do I hate discomfort, I also do not like to take unnecessary risks! I struggled the most in some seasons because I wanted the happy and simple path. I was so determined to stay positive that I didn't perform the due diligence necessary to identify risks.

Identifying risks in our journey is not a sign that we are failing or losing faith. This step is necessary to recognize our weaknesses, refine our strengths and stay on a path of growth. Failure to identify the risks and not properly mitigate them is a sign that one is likely to fail. Identifying and managing risks is vital to detecting and preventing defects or failures. Developing a risk plan helps to incorporate controls in your business plan to help mitigate losses.

It will help us to determine if we should pursue an academic degree, certifications, or acquire a special license. It helps us consider options for equipment investments, staff hires or contracting to a third party. By embracing risks, you become more prepared to handle the unexpected, and you also understand how fast you can really leap. Furthermore, understanding risks breeds gratefulness. It brings joy to the journey to witness what could have gone wrong and what should have happened, but didn't!

Review your business or career plan. What risks (reputational, financial, legal) could occur? What are the potential risks to your family, relationships, and even your health? How can you prevent or avoid the risks? If it does occur, what is your contingency plan?

_____

_____

_____

_____

_____

_____

_____

_____

_____

_____

_____

_____

_____

#8 Speak Affirmations to Yourself and Others

During a period when I was writing and preparing for several presentations, I had lunch with one of my sorority sisters. She asked what she could do to help me. I joked that she could get behind me and push! I needed people who would hold me accountable to what I said that I would do.

Well, writing slowed down. I was overwhelmed with life! One day, I received a short text from her inquiring about my progress and reminding me how special I am. She held me accountable, and in the process, her affirmation refueled my soul.

There will be seasons of your journey when you will feel low. It is inevitable. Reminding yourself of who you are and what you can accomplish will fuel you. You may want to share your concerns with a trusted friend(s) who can speak into you. Remember to also share affirmations with others. The power of delighting in others refuels the heart of the giver as well. As you look to be affirmed, give others what you hope to receive.

Try reading these affirmations aloud and often:

I am capable.
I deserve good things.
I am lovable.
I am powerful.
I am a life giver.
I am beautiful.
I am more than enough.
I am supposed to be here.
I am so proud of me.

What affirmations can you speak to others? Practice pouring into others daily and be amazed at what it does to refuel you, too.

#9 Be Careful Not to Carry Too Many Bags

We are all wounded people and have bags filled with past trauma. Do the work for your self-care by unpacking your bags with a trusted professional so that you may heal from past wounds and lighten your load. Forgive others, and do it often and quickly.

Forgiveness does not mean that you have to re-enter into a relationship with someone; but it does mean that you bless them to live well either on earth or in heaven, and you take back whatever joy, peace or power that he or she took from you. Whatever he or she did or said to you was wrong. But you have the choice not to take that person into your future.

You may need to forgive yourself for _____.

If it's difficult, that just means that you are human. Seek care through a counselor, life coach, spiritual director or trusted friend who can help you through the process. I have done the hard work to heal; consciously exposing my mind and heart to the pain in my soul. There were so many bags that I had buried under my work and false smiles that I had lost awareness of what was in the bags.

The result of telling my story has led me to a more grateful journey. In addition, it has freed me to live empowered, and my past pain is a source of healing for others. Carrying too many painful bags from the past slowed me down. None of us can leap if we are too burdened down.

It takes courage to reclaim what was lost or taken from you. Which wound has hurt the most? Which one has cost you the most joy and time? Identify someone today who can help you.

_____
_____
_____
_____
_____
_____
_____
_____

#10 Expect to Reach the Top

At some point in your journey, you will want to look back at the place where you began; but by that time, you will have climbed so high that it would take more effort to retreat than to continue climbing higher. In this stage of your journey, you no longer think the same. You have different expectations.

Keep moving, with the expectation that you will reach the top, and when you get there, keep moving to reach the next top. I believe that you can reach higher than you can even hope or dream – just keep going! Each step higher in the dream will challenge your capabilities and what you know and remind you that you are human. *If* you dare to explore the dream, the possibilities are as high as the leaps that you take.

Reflect on what you have accomplished. What's next? How will you celebrate your accomplishments along the way?

_____
_____
_____
_____
_____
_____
_____
_____
_____
_____

To reach our goals, we have to face our fears and learn something new. It may even require that we unlearn behaviors that are a hindrance to our success. Once we make the decision to travel the road to our dream, then we must not stop. If we begin the climb to something higher and stop, we will find ourselves stuck between a place that we no longer want to be in and a dream that no longer has hopeful possibilities. This stuck place will drain our joy and even promote chaos. This was a place that we were never supposed to remain and where we have now been way too long.

It is in this dissatisfied period that many will retreat to what is familiar. There is no progress, only an unfulfilled longing. A lost dream will devour something in our souls. We climb higher because something in our soul needs it. Something in each of us dies with our lost or deferred dream until there is new hope to inspire us to climb again.

For those who dare to take the LEAP, there is no retreat. The joy experienced in leaping breathes new life into our next opportunity and the next. The joy experienced in leaping sustains us as we learn to fall down and get back up again…and again and again, until we reach the goal. The joy experienced in leaping is transformative for the generations that we touch and for the generations that are watching to see what we are capable of and whether life will offer them hope for something more.

Each new possibility offers the challenge for us to lose something from the past that may be weighing us down. Taking the leap is not just about reaching the goals; it is about growing into our best selves, with the freedom to enjoy who we are and to enjoy the power of living in the light of this journey.

Building Your Platform
By Sharvette Mitchell

Don't sweat. Don't sweat.

Those words became my silent refrain that Saturday morning when I pulled into the partially completed parking lot of Aloft Hotel, located in the posh West End of Richmond, Virginia, also known as Short Pump. I knew that day – the very first time that I was visiting this hotel – that I would host an event here. In exactly twelve months, my premiere networking event would take place, and this had to be the location.

I loved the hotel's hip vibe, high-energy feel and eclectic design. It's not a big conference hotel and it's not a big business center. The Aloft has one conference room, an amazing lobby featuring clean and contemporary design aesthetics, and inviting areas for networking – the perfect setup for a boutique-style workshop or seminar.

Fast forward twelve months and that day had come. I was headlining my first event and it was at the Aloft Hotel in Short Pump. When I pulled into a parking space on the morning of July 26, 2014, however, rather than feeling excited or nervous, I found myself wrestling with fear, and even a little embarrassment. Because even though I was a social media superstar, with an enthusiastic and engaged list of followers, and a successful radio host with a dedicated listening audience and regular opportunities to interview celebrities, such as actress and gospel artist Tamela Mann from *Meet the Browns*, Thelma from *Good Times* (Bernadette Stanis), and Mama Joyce from the *Real Housewives of Atlanta*, and respected Christian leaders such as Pastor John Gray and Dr. Medina Pullings, on this day, I was setting up an event for just two people.

Yes, only two people had registered. Despite assurances from a business coach that based on my target audience, my first event – a social media master class for authors – would easily lure 15 to 20 people.

So here I found myself that morning, determined to put my best foot forward for these two attendees while not letting them see me sweat and mess up my makeup. I perspire easily, even if I am not nervous! On this day, the challenge was on...

I strolled into Aloft into my designated area with my retractable banner, laptop and the printed training materials that I had produced, prepared to give my two participants an excellent 2.5 hour training, all the while wondering why my efforts to reach more hadn't been successful. I had used a variety of strategies to promote the master class, from purchasing Facebook ads and creating fliers with eye-catching graphics to issuing email invitations and spreading the news word of mouth to authors I knew. I personally was aware of at least 10 authors who needed and could use my masterclass. But guess what? None of them registered and none of them attended.

As the hour neared for me to teach the two who had shown interest, I told myself to snap out of second guessing myself, but more questions arose, such as how was I going to explain to these two attendees that no one else had registered. What would they think of me and what would they think of this experience?

Well, a gentleman and a woman arrived, and guess what? They seemed unbothered that there weren't any other participants. I should mention that I even tried to give away a seat to an author that I know, and that morning I received a text message from her that she wasn't able to make it. So I was hoping for at least three in the room, but there we were, with two, and on we went with the masterclass.

Afterward, the gentleman walked up to me and let me know that he was the founder of a writer's group here in Richmond, Virginia. He wanted to know if I would come speak to the group. From that day forward, he has invited me to speak to his writer's group regularly and to speak at his annual conferences. All from a two person event.

Another interesting thing happened, or should I say did not happen, after my first event. I had been so worried, and even stressed, about what I would say when people asked, "How did it go? How did things turn out?" But no one asked. All the worrying that I did about having proof that I had this great event and having proof that I had these great people attend was all for nothing, because literally no one even asked me about the event.

Two years later, on the morning of my next live event, there I am, hanging out in the Hyatt House hotel in the West End/Short Pump area of Richmond, Virginia once again. It's 7 a.m. and I'm having my makeup done to prepare for a conference with 75 registered attendees who are arriving and assembling downstairs in the Vineyard conference room. I am grateful, I'm thankful, and I'm a little anxious. I start thinking about my first event, at the Aloft hotel with two people, and questioning what changed in my business and brand between the first event and this second event to go from two to 75 registered guests.

The best answer I could come up with is that I propelled my brand forward by focusing on the things that build your personal brand. Yes, I had web design clients, radio show listeners, likes and comments; but what I realized was that I did not have community. So I started focusing on building my platform, personal brand and my influence. Those things propelled my business forward, and ultimately, propelled my events forward.

You see, building your platform will help you establish credibility and authority in your target market and eventually convert social media likes into customers and supporters. People buy from those that are credible and from those that they perceive are leaders. Building your platform will take you from where you are to where you dream of being. Adopting that mindset and following through with consistent strategies propelled my business forward to the point that I could walk away from a very comfortable job in which I was thriving to pursue my visions, pursue my dreams, and pursue my business full-time.

If you're sitting there and you're saying, "I need to change the trajectory of my life and of my business and of my brand," I want to share with you six components that helped me build my brand and platform, which in turn has propelled me forward.

Let's jump in! I worked on my 1) Visual Branding 2) Products and Services 3) Media Exposure 4) Speaking Opportunities 5) Books And 6) Events. Over the next few pages, I will peel back the covers and share key points around these six components. If you implement them, they will propel you forward as well.

VISUAL BRANDING

In many cases, consumers assess your value and expertise based on what they see. The visual part of your brand is important so that it does not distract, and instead attracts, your ideal customers. Your visual branding consists of brand colors, professional photography, a logo, website/landing page, business cards, social media graphics, flyers, etc. You should start with identifying two to five brand colors, which will be used consistently in ALL of your visual branding. Let's look at Target. Their brand colors, red and white, are interwoven throughout their stores, on their website, on shopping carts and shopping bags. It does not matter if the Target is in Richmond, Virginia, Atlanta, Georgia or Seattle, Washington – the brand colors are consistent.

The next critical component is professional photography. To propel your brand forward, you need professional pictures of yourself and your products. It's true that a picture is worth a thousand words. Communicate what you and your business bring to the table through photography. Make sure you wear your brand colors at your photo shoot!

We can't leave social media out of this conversation. Many customers find out about your brand from interactions (i.e. posts, graphics, videos, comments, etc.) on social media. This is often your first chance to make a first impression, and first impressions are lasting. Your social media graphics should be in your brand colors and include your professional photography and or professional stock photos. Use your social media to highlight how you help clients solve problems through the services and products you offer.

The last key component of your visual brand is your website. This is your communication and marketing hub on the world wide web and fully showcases what your clients can purchase and the solutions you offer clients. Your website visually tells the marketplace your brand promise and enables your business and brand to propel forward and generate more revenue.

PRODUCTS AND SERVICES

As entrepreneurs, our goal is to generate revenue. We do that by consistently offering products and services. If you are finding it hard to make money, look at what you offer. Are you giving away your gifts and talents? Some new entrepreneurs fall in to the pit of failing to charge for their services but you can't do that anymore! It stops today. You have spent too much time and energy to gain the expertise you have, and you deserve to be paid for that.

The next question is...do you offer enough? What do I mean by enough? Some clients want your high-end products and services, but there may be customers who need a lower-priced product or service as an introduction to your brand. On the flip side, your current products and services may all be on the lower end, giving you opportunities to create and offer VIP or high-end options. For example, I offer digital products for as low as $20, but coaching and web design services cost several thousand. Once you have your products and services evaluated and updated, you must consistently market them! Getting and keeping attention on your products and services draws attention to your overall brand, and this will continue to propel you forward.

MEDIA EXPOSURE

Most brands crave media attention. Who does not want to be featured on TV, radio, in magazines or in newspapers? Yourdictionary.com defines a media outlet as "a publication or broadcast program that provides news and feature stories to the public through various distribution channels."

Traditional media outlets have historically included newspapers, magazines, radio, television, and the Internet. The good news is that by today's societal standards, the term "media" now encompasses even more outlets – many of which are easily accessible by entrepreneurs and small business owners. We can add in blogs, podcasts, Internet radio, YouTube channels and shows, online magazines, and more to the list. This variety of options gives you new opportunities to get in front of someone else's audience and propel your brand forward. It may be cool and sexy to get featured on ABC, NBC and CBS; however, don't disdain coverage on web-based media or on your local radio and TV programing. Online blogs and magazines are always looking for quotes and input from experts. Check out helpareporter.com to get started.

If you don't interview well locally, you will make a mess of things when you get the "big" opportunities. Follow and connect with local TV and radio personalities to be considered for mention. My first time on CBS6 was to discuss my second conference. I got that opportunity because I established and maintained a relationship with a local media personality. (Let me stick a pin here: Establish genuine relationships, because people can read through fake connections. Also, always nurture the connection from the angle of how you can help the media contact and not just the other way around. Jumping off my soapbox now!)

The flip side of seeking media attention is that you can become media. Consider hosting your own podcast or YouTube show and interview guests. This adds a celebrity factor to your brand!

SPEAKING

According to Magneticspeaking.com, 75% of the U.S. population fears public speaking. That's about 27 million Americans! When you speak, or embed speaking as a component of your brand, that automatically propels you beyond 27 million people.

Finding and creating speaking opportunities are key to building your platform. Speaking at conferences, workshops, seminars, events, churches, etc., puts you and your services and products in front of new audiences. This is critical to increasing your revenue and exposure, because you always need a new flow of people getting a chance to experience your brand.

You establish rapport with others the quickest when you are in person. Social media is great, and email is wonderful; but there is nothing like being in a room with potential customers. You also have a higher conversion rate when you have a live interaction with potential clients. Let me ask you a question: If I needed you to come on a stage right now to speak, with no preparation, what

THREE topics could you discuss? Take a minute and write those down. These topics are a starting point for creating your "signature talks." Yes, you may find that you will tweak and customize your signature talks according to the speaking engagement, but at the end of the day, you can flow with your area of expertise.

BOOKS

Word on the street is that a book is the new business card. I am not sure if I completely believe that; however, I do believe being a published author or co-author adds credibility to your brand and platform. Consumers pay more for services and products that they deem are from an expert. Many events and conferences like to feature experts and speakers who have books. Even local and national media often interview guest authors who can share expert insight on a news story.

In fact, of the 500 hundred-plus people I have interviewed for my podcast, *The Sharvette Mitchell Radio Show*, 60% of the guests had a book. And guess what? The average consumer considers an author to be a celebrity. This is partially due to movies and media that portray authors living a glamorous lifestyle, sitting at the beach writing their books from their summer cottages. That may not be your situation, but the fact remains that when you publish a book, it propels the perception of your brand forward.

Perhaps writing an entire book seems daunting – and it is! Consider other options, as I did, such as participating in anthologies or book collaborations. Partner with others and share your expertise together. In business, we are writing all of the time, whether for our website, blog or social media, or in emails and other correspondence; so you probably have a great starting point right under your nose!

EVENTS

This chapter opened with me describing the journey to my first event, and how I persisted despite modest turnout. Now, I'd like to share what I regret about that first event. It has nothing to do with just two people registering, with the venue, or even the marketing. What I regret is my perception of that first event – how I initially considered it a failure, and as a result, waited almost two years before hosting another.

What if I'd had a different mindset and jumped back in the saddle two months later, with a goal of registering four to six people? What if I then tried for eight or ten registrants four months later? What if....? Instead, I allowed fear to hold me back for 24 months.

This is what I can unequivocally tell you: Hosting my own conferences and workshops has changed the trajectory of my brand and propelled me forward. That's why you must include events as a component to your brand and business. You might be wondering where you start and how much it is going to cost. Start small. An event does not mean a two-day conference like my conference. It could be a two-hour workshop in a local restaurant that has a private room. There are many facilities (outside of hotels) that would love to have small business owners come in and host events.

Your next question may be *Will anyone buy tickets or register?* The answer is YES –particularly if you have worked on the other five components of building your platform. Here is a key point that some miss: Your event (big or small) should draw the attention of your ideal client. The amount of people registered is not as important as attracting your ideal client. What's more important is a captive and qualified audience of raving fans that are, or will become, customers!

So perhaps hosting your own event is not where you are right now. Guess what? You can leverage and attend others' events and get some of the same results. Be a vendor or a sponsor for someone else's event, which allows your brand to gain exposure with different people. You should also network, so that you can grow and learn business strategies. You don't need to be the superstar speaker or celebrity expert on the stage to benefit from an event. You will be surprised at the shoulders you will rub if you are sitting in the RIGHT rooms.

Wow, that's a lot, right? Even so, you don't need to work on all of the components at the same time. Select an area of focus and work that bad boy until the wheels fall off. After that, move to the next component of building your personal brand and your platform.

It may be best to work with an expert on these components. Let's grab a virtual cup of tea and have a "meet and greet" to discuss some solutions for you. Simply jump onto www.CallSharvette.com. I am here to help entrepreneurs who struggle with attracting attention and exposure for their brand and who want to build their online platform. Clients who work with me generate more revenue and increase brand awareness to propel to the next phase, in life and business. Whatever route you choose, just get started.

MEET THE AUTHORS

Sharvette Mitchell

Sharvette Mitchell is a graduate of Virginia Commonwealth University with a Bachelor of Science in Marketing. She brings to the table, 25 years past experience in corporate America in the field of training & development and Consumer Compliance. Sharvette provides web design services for entrepreneurs so that they can generate more revenue with an amazing online brand. In conjunction to web design, Sharvette is a Consultant & Trainer and conducts training and seminars with an emphasis on the use of Facebook marketing, personal branding strategies and creation of digital products. She is a Professional Certified Leadership Coach and on the Board of Directors of James River Writers.

Sharvette is a past recipient of the Richmond Star Award, ACHI Magazine's – Radio Personality of The Year Award and has been featured in publications such as Huffington Post, HOPE for Women Magazine, DIVA By Design Magazine, CEO Magazine, Glambitious Magazine, Rescue A CEO Blog & Sista Sense Magazine. Sharvette has also been seen on CBS 6 Virginia This Morning, The CW Network and Comcast Cable. Since 2008, she has hosted a weekly talk radio show, The Sharvette Mitchell Radio Show, that airs on Blog Talk Radio, iTunes and on her personal mobile app. Lastly, Sharvette is the visionary author of the anthology, PROPEL and a co-author in two books, Mogul In the Making and Get It Done! Design The Business of Your Dreams. Find more out at www.Mitchell-Productions.com

Althea Simpson

Althea Simpson, MBA, LCSW, LICSW is an independent business consultant with over 15 years' experience in the business arena. Althea also has nine years' experience as a Licensed Clinical Social Worker, specializing in trauma recovery. She has been consulting with individuals and small businesses for more than eight years.

Althea helps individuals and companies create "success stories" that they can execute well and align activities with key strategies. She advises on and provides training and coaching in the areas of mental health, strategic and change management, marketing and client relationship management. Althea walks-the-walk, serving many roles in the mental health and business communities and is committed to helping others improve business practices.

Eulica Kimber

Eulica Kimber has been speaking and teaching the language of business, accounting, for over 25 years. As a Certified Public Accountant (CPA) and Master of Business Administration (MBA), her education and professional experience in accounting and entrepreneurship have given her the ability to help her clients by removing the fear and intimidation of the financial aspects of their businesses. She does this by creating customized action plans for the startup and growth of businesses through her online Plan2Pro$per Small Business Academy and one on one business coaching.

Learn more about Eulica and her services at www.eulicakimbercpa.com.

Laticia Austin

Laticia Austin is a serial entrepreneur. She has worked in the technology industry for 20+ years, transforming companies and providing organizational change management. She currently operates Austin & Associates, a technology consulting firm that has worked with many organizations found on the Fortune 50 list. During her command at Austin & Associates, LLC, she started yet another venture, 123JobZone. This brainchild is a job board catering to small and medium-sized businesses. Her latest entrepreneurial journey is a mobile app development company, My Brand. My App.

Laticia is one to always stay relevant. She understands the needs of her clients and pushes forward to give them exactly what they need. Her tough love approach garners stunning results for those that trust the systems she has created for success. If you are trying to navigate the technology space, you don't have to do it alone.

Contact Laticia today at www.MyBrandMyApp.com.

Dr. Amy Walton

Amy Walton, also known as "Dr Amy", is a speaker, coach, and change agent, who educates, equips, and empowers women to bust through the obstacles that hold their faith and financial goals hostage so they can free themselves to live life on their terms, build their businesses, and reach their faith and financial goals. She is an ordained minister of the Gospel of Jesus Christ. She holds an undergraduate degree in Psychology, a Master of Arts in Human Services with a specialization in Executive Leadership, and a Doctorate of Ministry in Christian Leadership. She is currently pursuing a Doctorate of Education in Community Care and Counseling through Liberty University in Lynchburg, Virginia.

Visit www.dramywalton.com

Sheryll Golden

A native of Ohio, Sheryll spent many years employed in the healthcare arena and has always had a deep yearning to make a difference in the world. She obtained her Nursing degree in 1997 and then a MSN in 2013. She spent 16 years in pediatrics, loving the difference she could make for so many little patients and families. At some point, her love of makeup and skincare got her involved in a little Mary Kay business to have fun and make some side money. It was there she realized she could make an impact in a different way.

She is now an Image Consultant and fulfills her passion of helping women feel more confident with skincare and makeup. Now living in Richmond, VA she is married to her husband Fred (who is a proud Canadian). Together they enjoy travelling, exploring all types of restaurants, breweries and wineries. At home they enjoy relaxing, watching movies and TV series and giving treats to their two cats Sid and Sookie.

Sandra Hayashi

As a busy professional, you need to partner with a REALTOR® that will be available to answer your calls and guide you through the process of purchasing your new home. Sandra works with her clients to always be available when needed. She understands that everyone's schedule varies, so whether you need to see a home on the weekend or after 5:00 p.m. during the week, she's available to answer your call. Sandra is passionate about educating her clients throughout the process and easing any anxiety they might feel about buying a home.

Sandra grew up in Colonial Heights and has lived in Chester for the last 30 years. She loves the area and it has been a wonderful place to raise her children. As a child, there was freedom to play in the streets without worrying about crime and she believes much of that comfort still exists today. It is her pleasure to continue introducing people to the community that she has loved for over 30 years and help them find a place to call home.

Yolanda Gray

Yolanda Gray is a faith-based mentor, speaker and author of abundant living for women who feel trapped on the hamster wheel that has become their life. She shows you how to get out of the stress and overwhelm and Take Back Your Life! for the one God created you for—authentically and confidently. She uses her education, life experience and Biblical principles in coaching, teaching and speaking with Jesus' love, Holy Spirit's energy and wisdom, and God's power. Most importantly, she leads you to living life loved. Because when you know God's love everything changes and anything is possible. Yolanda earned a B.S. in Human Development, an M.A. in Human Relations from Liberty University and certified as a holistic life coach.

Website: www.yolandagray.com
Email: Yolanda@yolandagray.com.
You can join her free Facebook Group #takebackyourlife!

Cynthia Williams-Bey

Mrs. Williams-Bey is the visionary and CEO of not just 1 but several businesses. She is the founder of Heaven Sent Child Care LLC, Heaven Sent Childcare To You, Spring Forth LLC and Co-Owner of Dream Productions Inc. As a seasoned CEO. of 14+yrs, she consults and coaches aspiring and current business owners as well as offers strategic planning for business recovery and bottom line increase.

Born and raised in Bedford Stuyvesant Brooklyn she was counted out by society so she decided to count herself back in and help others do the same. Mrs. Williams-Bey is a Wife, Mother of 6, Community Leader, Award-winning Author, and International Speaker.

To learn more follow her on social media @mrswilliamsbey and visit her website @ www.mrswilliamsbey.com.

Monica M. Bijoux

Monica M. Bijoux is the founder and CEO of DECIDE TO MOVE, LLC (DTM), and has been coaching business owners, entrepreneurs, and individuals for over 15 years. She also has been working with veterans as they transition from active duty life to business owners and entrepreneurs for the last 10 years. Monica has a Master of Science Administration with a concentration in Human Resources and a Master of Social Work. These degrees have allowed her to combine her passion for helping individuals find their authentic self and work to their highest potential while combining her business mindset. She also combines a variety of special trainings; Certified Coaching, Hypnotherapy, Emotion Freedom Technique, Neuro-linguistic Programming, and Emotional Intelligence to assist in helping her clients.

Learn more at www.DecideToMove.com.

Pastor Annie Theresa Bryant Fields

Pastor Annie Theresa Bryant Fields is the pastor of Abundant Peace Ministries located in Jacksonville, FL. After God, her family is the LOVE of her life! In addition to serving in the kingdom, Pastor Fields has been an educator for over 29 years in both the public and private sector. She was named 2003-2004 Clay County Teacher of The Year, making her the first and still today the only African-American to win the prestigious award in Clay County.

Pastor Fields is also the owner and CEO of PEACE In Jewels, LLC, whereas she has the opportunity to showcase her passion for exquisite accessories. One of Pastor Fields greatest desires is to make a difference in other people lives by leading, equipping and empowering them to accomplish phenomenal things in life. She makes it a point to accomplish this with unconditional love, genuine extraordinary methods and life-changing words from God.

Reverend Dr. Marlene Fuller

Reverend Dr. Marlene Fuller is the pastor of Pleasant Grove Baptist Church in Mechanicsville, VA. Dr. Fuller is the owner and director of LEAP, LLC where she provides counseling, spiritual direction, and life coaching to individuals and small groups. Dr. Fuller graduated from The College of William and Mary with a Bachelor of Arts in Sociology and Theatre/Speech, an MBA from Averett University, a Master of Divinity from the Samuel DeWitt Proctor School of Theology at Virginia Union University and earned a Doctor of Ministry in Formational Counseling from Ashland Theological Seminary. Additionally, she is a Vice-President in Project Management at Citizens Bank.

Her greatest passion is positioning others for healing; helping them to identify areas of broken-ness and break-free of the bondage of old wounds so they can transform and experience an abundant life.

Dr. Fuller can be reached at www.marlenefuller.com.

www.ingramcontent.com/pod-product-compliance
Lightning Source LLC
Chambersburg PA
CBHW052050070526
44584CB00017B/2121